CONTEMPORARY'S

Practical English Writing Skills

A Handbook with PRACTICE

Second Edition

Mona Scheraga

CONTEMPORARY BOOKS

a division of NTC/CONTEMPORARY PUBLISHING GROUP
Lincolnwood, Illinois USA

To my mother and father,
Jean and Ben Liechenstein,
whose faith and encouragement have made it all possible.

ISBN: 0-8092-0453-3

Acknowledgments begin on page iv, which is to be considered an extension of this
copyright page.

Published by Contemporary Books,
a division of NTC/Contemporary Publishing Group, Inc.,
4255 West Touhy Avenue,
Lincolnwood (Chicago), Illinois 60646-1975 U.S.A.

3 4 5 6 7 8 9 VGRVGR 10 9 8 7 6 5 4 3 2 1

Contents

Practical English Writing Skills

Acknowledgments

Working with Becky Rauff, my editor on the original project, with Mary Jane Maples, my "revision" editor and purveyor of great ideas and humor, and with editor Paula Eacott of the intimidating credentials has been a special privilege. Their patience, insight, and expertise cannot be overestimated. The thousands of students who passed through my classes in more than twenty-five years of teaching deserve a special thanks. Each, in turn, helped fine-tune my understanding of the infinite dimensions of the teaching/learning process. To my husband, Murray, for being confidant and adviser, artist and proofreader, and chief cook and pot scrubber during the revising of this text, go the thanks of an extremely grateful if sometimes neglectful wife.

I really must thank the profession, English as a second/foreign language, for the friends I've made in the field. To Professor Alice Jiménez, former Special Assistant to the Secretary of Education of Puerto Rico, and a very special friend, my thanks for her incisive comments and suggestions as she read portions of the original work in progress. For their advice and support, too, go thanks to Connie Attanasio, who can always be counted on, and to the many teachers in Clark County Las Vegas and New York City, in particular, whose suggestions have inspired the additions found in the revised edition of *Practical English Writing Skills*.

I am grateful to Northwestern University, Evanston, Illinois, for allowing us to reprint a Northwestern Application for Admission; to William Paterson University, Wayne, New Jersey, for allowing us to reprint a William Paterson University Application for Admission; and to TOPS Business Forms, Lisle, Illinois, for permission to use two of their job application forms. Special thanks, too, to Kathy Blattner for allowing me to use her fascinating term paper on the Amish.

I would like to acknowledge all the people I have worked with and learned from over the years. I am not unaware of how lucky I am to have been exposed to so many meaningful experiences in and out of the classroom.

Introduction

Practical English Writing Skills is a guide to developing the writing skills we all need to function and succeed in our everyday lives—at home, on the job, and in school. Each type of writing is discussed and explained in a straightforward, helpful way; treating everyday tasks with as much respect as the more academic skills.

Practical English Writing Skills is for high school, junior college, and adult education limited-English students. It is also for English as a foreign language students planning to live/work/function in an English-speaking environment, and for the many native speakers of English who need help mastering a variety of basic writing skills too often ignored in today's classrooms. The format of the book also makes *Practical English Writing Skills* suitable for independent study, for students who want to improve their writing skills on their own without a formal language program.

For each type of writing, you will find:

1. a **Rationale** for doing this type of writing

2. a list of the **Materials Needed**

3. the **Skills Involved**

4. the **Important Vocabulary**

5. an **Example** of the kind of writing to be practiced

6. a step-by-step **Procedure** for doing the writing and

7. a **Practice** activity—a real-life task involving the kind of writing that's been discussed.

In addition, most of the lessons include an evaluation process to measure the success of the written practice.

Practical English Writing Skills is meant to be used as it best suits the user. Therefore, you can start at page one and follow through to the end; start in the middle and work backward and forward at will; or even start with the last chapter, if that's the one you need immediately. No matter where you begin, you will find that *Practical English Writing Skills* is not only a guide but also an easy reference book, much the same as your dictionary. You can turn to this book anytime for information about whatever type of writing you need to do. The book was written with your needs in mind. Enjoy.

Unit One

Job Applications and Résumés

Filling Out a Job Application

F ew people go through life without ever having to fill out a job application. There may be many job applications in your future, or there may be only one. In either case, filling out a job application is not a difficult thing to do, but doing it right is extremely important.

Rationale

Job applications ask for all the information employers want to know about people before deciding whether to interview them. The way you answer the questions on the job application may determine whether or not you are called back for an interview or considered for a job. Therefore, it is important to know how to fill out an application correctly.

Note: Federal (United States) laws prohibit employers from requiring job applicants to answer certain questions. These include questions about age, race, sex, marital status, dependents, and other questions of a personal nature. If these questions appear on an application, you must decide whether to answer them or not. Some companies, especially those directly involved with the government, are allowed to ask these questions for a variety of security reasons. However, most employers today are careful to use applications that protect the rights and privacy of people applying for jobs.

Materials Needed

pen, practice paper, job application, dictionary, information about your educational background and work experience, names and addresses of references

Skills Involved

reading comprehension; spelling; neat and legible handwriting; compiling and organizing information

Important Vocabulary

compiling collecting

dependents people who rely on someone else for support. Children and others who can't work or earn money are dependents.

employee a person who works for someone else

employer a company or person for whom others work

hiring giving someone a job

marital status whether you are married, single, divorced, or widowed

personal relating to your private life. Your marital status is personal information; your job skills are not.

personnel office / human resources office the department within a company that is responsible for hiring, firing, and dealing with employee benefits and problems

potential possible

references people who know you and can provide information about your qualifications and the kind of person you are

supervisor a person in charge of other employees

Example

See next page.

APPLICATION FOR EMPLOYMENT
(PRE-EMPLOYMENT QUESTIONNAIRE)   (AN EQUAL OPPORTUNITY EMPLOYER)

PERSONAL INFORMATION

DATE 12/1/98

NAME Stein   Suzanne   E.
LAST   FIRST   MIDDLE

SOCIAL SECURITY NUMBER 111-11-1111

PRESENT ADDRESS 8 Elm St.   Brownsville   TX   78520
STREET   CITY   STATE   ZIP

PERMANENT ADDRESS same as above
CITY   STATE   ZIP

PHONE NO. (210)555-6666   ARE YOU 18 YEARS OR OLDER Yes ☒ No ☐

SPECIAL QUESTIONS

DO NOT ANSWER **ANY** OF THE QUESTIONS IN THIS FRAMED AREA UNLESS THE EMPLOYER HAS **CHECKED** A **BOX PRECEDING** A QUESTION, THEREBY INDICATING THAT THE INFORMATION IS REQUIRED FOR A BONA FIDE OCCUPATIONAL QUALIFICATION, OR DICTATED BY NATIONAL SECURITY LAWS, OR IS NEEDED FOR OTHER LEGALLY PERMISSIBLE REASONS.

☐ Height _____ feet _____ inches

☐ Weight _____ lbs.

☐ What Foreign Languages do you speak fluently? _____

☐ _____

☐ Citizen of U.S. ____ Yes ____ No

☐ Date of Birth* _____

____ Read _____ Write _____

*The Age Discrimination in Employment Act of 1967 prohibits discrimination on the basis of age with respect to individuals who are at least 40 but less than 70 years of age.

EMPLOYMENT DESIRED

POSITION salesperson

DATE YOU CAN START 1/3/99

SALARY DESIRED open

ARE YOU EMPLOYED NOW? yes

IF SO MAY WE INQUIRE OF YOUR PRESENT EMPLOYER? yes

EVER APPLIED TO THIS COMPANY BEFORE? no   WHERE? ——   WHEN? ——

EDUCATION	NAME AND LOCATION OF SCHOOL	*NO. OF YEARS ATTENDED	*DID YOU GRADUATE?	SUBJECTS STUDIED
GRAMMAR SCHOOL	No. 6 School, Carrol St., Paterson, N.J	8	yes	
HIGH SCHOOL	Brownsville High School Brownsville, TX	4	yes	English, science, math, business
COLLEGE				
TRADE, BUSINESS OR CORRESPONDENCE SCHOOL	Haley's Correspondence School for Sales, Chicago, IL	1	yes	how to be a top salesperson

*The Age Discrimination in Employment Act of 1967 prohibits discrimination on the basis of age with respect to individuals who are at least 40 but less than 70 years of age.

GENERAL

SUBJECTS OF SPECIAL STUDY OR RESEARCH WORK   sales

U.S. MILITARY OR NAVAL SERVICE ——   RANK ——

PRESENT MEMBERSHIP IN NATIONAL GUARD OR RESERVES ——

TOPS FORM 3285 (REVISED)   (CONTINUED ON OTHER SIDE)   LITHO IN U.S.A.

FORMER EMPLOYERS [LIST BELOW LAST FOUR EMPLOYERS, STARTING WITH LAST ONE FIRST].

DATE MONTH AND YEAR	NAME AND ADDRESS OF EMPLOYER	SALARY	POSITION	REASON FOR LEAVING
FROM Sept. 1996 TO present	Jones Department Store 1 Main St., Brownsville, TX	$25,000	sales	to improve and advance
FROM TO				
FROM TO				
FROM TO				

REFERENCES: GIVE THE NAMES OF THREE PERSONS NOT RELATED TO YOU, WHOM YOU HAVE KNOWN AT LEAST ONE YEAR.

NAME	ADDRESS	BUSINESS	YEARS ACQUAINTED
1 Rev. C. Smythe	15 Elmora Rd. Brownsville, TX	clergy	10
2 Mr. R. Jones	Jones Dept. Store 1 Main St., Brownsville, TX	owner	2
3 Mrs. J. Méndez	555 6th Ave. Brownsville, TX	store manager	2

PHYSICAL RECORD:

DO YOU HAVE ANY PHYSICAL LIMITATIONS THAT PRECLUDE YOU FROM PERFORMING ANY WORK FOR WHICH YOU ARE BEING CONSIDERED? ☐ Yes ☒ No

PLEASE DESCRIBE:

IN CASE OF EMERGENCY NOTIFY Mr. J. Stein   8 Elm St., Brownsville, TX   (210) 555-6666
NAME   ADDRESS   PHONE NO.

"I CERTIFY THAT THE FACTS CONTAINED IN THIS APPLICATION ARE TRUE AND COMPLETE TO THE BEST OF MY KNOWLEDGE AND UNDERSTAND THAT, IF EMPLOYED, FALSIFIED STATEMENTS ON THIS APPLICATION SHALL BE GROUNDS FOR DISMISSAL.

I AUTHORIZE INVESTIGATION OF ALL STATEMENTS CONTAINED HEREIN AND THE REFERENCES LISTED ABOVE TO GIVE YOU ANY AND ALL INFORMATION CONCERNING MY PREVIOUS EMPLOYMENT AND ANY PERTINENT INFORMATION THEY MAY HAVE, PERSONAL OR OTHERWISE, AND RELEASE ALL PARTIES FROM ALL LIABILITY FOR ANY DAMAGE THAT MAY RESULT FROM FURNISHING SAME TO YOU.

I UNDERSTAND AND AGREE THAT, IF HIRED, MY EMPLOYMENT IS FOR NO DEFINITE PERIOD AND MAY, REGARDLESS OF THE DATE OF PAYMENT OF MY WAGES AND SALARY, BE TERMINATED AT ANY TIME WITHOUT ANY PRIOR NOTICE."

DATE 12/1/98   SIGNATURE *Suzanne E. Stein*

DO NOT WRITE BELOW THIS LINE

INTERVIEWED BY _____ DATE _____

_____

HIRED: ☐ Yes   ☐ No   POSITION _____   DEPT. _____

SALARY/WAGE _____   DATE REPORTING TO WORK _____

APPROVED: 1. _____ 2. _____ 3. _____
EMPLOYMENT MANAGER   DEPT. HEAD   GENERAL MANAGER

This form has been designed to strictly comply with State and Federal fair employment practice laws prohibiting employment discrimination. This Application for Employment Form is sold for general use throughout the United States. TOPS assumes no responsibility for the inclusion in said form of any questions which, when asked by the Employer of the Job Applicant, may violate State and/or Federal Law.

Procedure ▼

1. Read the application carefully. Be sure to follow the directions.

   a. Use a pen to fill in your answers (unless you are asked to type).
   b. Look up any words you don't understand in a dictionary or ask someone to explain their meaning. Never be ashamed to say you don't understand something.

2. If there are any questions that require a paragraph or longer answer, write your answer on separate paper first so you can correct it before you put it on the application.

3. Look at the example application again. Note these important details and watch for them whenever you fill out an application.

   a. *Name:* Last name should be written first.
   b. *Address:* If you are presently living or staying somewhere other than at your permanent address, be sure to include that information. Your current address is necessary for an employer to get in touch with you to set up an interview.
   c. *Special Questions:* Follow the directions, and don't answer these questions unless you are specifically asked to do so.
   d. *Employment Desired:* If you don't want your present employer to know you are looking for another job, ask that he or she not be contacted—at least until you have been interviewed and there is a possibility you will be hired.
   e. *Salary Desired:* If you are not sure what salary you want, or if you want to hear what's available, write *open* in this blank. That means you are willing to discuss this item with the interviewer.
   f. *Education:* Notice that the years you attended or graduated from particular schools are not asked for, just the number of years you attended each school. This protects you from revealing your age.
   g. *Former Employers:* Be sure to follow the directions and to put your most recent employer first. When listing reasons for leaving a job, it is always best to be positive; you are seeking to improve yourself, your salary, etc. Personal motives such as not liking your boss are not good reasons to leave a job in the eyes of future employers.
   h. Draw a line through any spaces that don't apply to you to show that you have read the question, but that it doesn't affect you.
   i. Read everything carefully before you sign the application, and be sure you understand what you are agreeing to.

Practice ▼

Now it's your turn.

Task:　to fill out a job application

Situation:　You are applying for a job of your choice. Fill out the application on the following page. Remember to read it first and be sure you understand everything before filling it in.

APPLICATION FOR EMPLOYMENT
(PRE-EMPLOYMENT QUESTIONNAIRE)   (AN EQUAL OPPORTUNITY EMPLOYER)

Date _____

Name [Last Name First] _____   Soc. Sec. No. _____

Address _____   Telephone _____

What kind of work are you applying for? _____

What special qualifications do you have? _____

What office machines can you operate? _____

Are you 18 years or older?   Yes _____   No _____

SPECIAL PURPOSE QUESTIONS

DO NOT ANSWER **ANY** OF THE QUESTIONS IN THIS FRAMED AREA UNLESS THE EMPLOYER HAS **CHECKED A BOX PRECEDING** A QUESTION, THEREBY INDICATING THAT THE INFORMATION IS REQUIRED FOR A BONA FIDE OCCUPATIONAL QUALIFICATION, OR DICTATED BY NATIONAL SECURITY LAWS, OR IS NEEDED FOR OTHER LEGALLY PERMISSIBLE REASONS.

☐ Height ____Feet ____Inches ☐ Weight _____Lbs. ☐ Are you prevented from lawfully being employed in the U.S.? Yes____ No____

☐ Have you been convicted of a felony or misdemeanor within the last 5 years?* Yes_____ No_____ Describe _____

*You will not be denied employment solely because of a conviction record, unless the offense is related to the job for which you have applied.

MILITARY SERVICE RECORD

Armed Forces Service _____ Yes _____ No

Branch of Service _____ Duties _____

Rank or rating at time of enlistment _____ Rating at time of discharge _____

Do you have any physical limitations that prohibit you from performing any work for which you are being considered? Yes____ No____

If yes, what can be done to accommodate your limitation? Describe _____

EDUCATION

SCHOOL	*NO. OF YEARS ATTENDED	NAME OF SCHOOL	CITY	COURSE	*DID YOU GRADUATE?
GRAMMAR					
HIGH					
COLLEGE					
OTHER					

*The Age Discrimination in Employment Act of 1967 prohibits discrimination on the basis of age with respect to individuals who are at least 40 but less than 70 years of age.

EXPERIENCE

NAME AND ADDRESS OF COMPANY	DATE FROM	DATE TO	LIST YOUR DUTIES	STARTING SALARY	FINAL SALARY	REASON FOR LEAVING

BUSINESS REFERENCES

NAME	ADDRESS	OCCUPATION

This form has been designed to strictly comply with State and Federal fair employment practice laws prohibiting employment discrimination. This Application for Employment Form is sold for general use throughout the United States. TOPS assumes no responsibility for the inclusion in said form of any questions which, when asked by the Employer of the Job Applicant, may violate State and/or Federal Law.

TOPS Form 3286 (84-3)   Litho in U.S.A.

2

Writing a Résumé

A résumé is a summary of your qualifications—in particular, your work experience and educational background. Your first job, at "entry-level", may not require a résumé. However, as your skills, work experience, and salary needs increase, you will need to begin sending a résumé to potential employers.

Rationale

People in charge of personnel departments usually ask for résumés from job applicants and then contact the applicants whose résumés show the best qualifications for the type of job involved. If your résumé shows that you have the skills and background an employer is looking for, and if it's neat and professional in appearance, you may be asked to go in for an interview.

Note: As you go from job to job, it's a good idea to keep a record of the exact names and addresses of the places you've worked, who your supervisor(s) were, and the dates of your employment there. This makes it easier to keep your résumé up-to-date.

Materials Needed

typewriter or word processor, unlined paper, access to a copying machine, names, addresses, and dates of places you've worked and schools you've attended, practice paper, pen or pencil

Skills Involved

organizing material; planning a layout for a résumé; using correct spelling, punctuation, and capitalization; typing or word processing

Important Vocabulary

employee a person who works for someone else

employer a company or person for whom others work

employment a job

entry-level beginning level; requiring little or no experience

layout a plan for the way something will look

marital status whether you are married, single, divorced, or widowed

personnel department the department in a company that is responsible for hiring, firing, and dealing with employee benefits and problems

potential possible

references people who know you and can provide information about your qualifications and the kind of person you are

supervisor a person in charge of other employees

Example

See next page.

OLGA ORTIZ
400 Lane Drive
Albany, New York   12234
518-555-1234

CAREER OBJECTIVE

Full-time position as a bilingual aide/teacher in a public school.

WORK EXPERIENCE

Sept. 1997–Present   Bilingual Aide   Marsh Adult School
1 Market St.
Albany, NY   12234

Work with new Spanish-speaking arrivals, helping them to register for English classes.

EDUCATION

June 1997:   AA Degree   Passaic County Community College
College Blvd.
Paterson, NJ   07501

June 1995:   Diploma   Passaic High School
Passaic, NJ   07055

HONORS AND ACTIVITIES

Certificate of Merit in Spanish (Passaic High School)
Perfect Attendance Award (Passaic High School)
President, French Club (Passaic County Community College)

SKILLS

Multilingual (fluent in English, Spanish, and French)

REFERENCES

Mr. K. Bodnar, Chair
English Dept.
Passaic High School
Passaic, NJ   07055

Prof. L. Smith
Passaic County Community College
College Blvd.
Paterson, NJ   07501

Dr. J. Mendez, Director
Marsh Adult School
1 Market St.
Albany, NY   12234

Procedure ▼

There are many acceptable ways to write a résumé. The format (layout) used here is one popular style that is easy to read, pleasing to look at, and contains the necessary information. The laws of the United States protect you from having to state your marital status, age, number of dependents, race, or sex on your résumé.

1. At the top of the paper, center your name, address, and telephone number. Use single spacing as shown below. A résumé should always be typed, typeset, or done on a word processor.

> Donald Lovrin
> 109 Simpson Blvd.
> Los Angeles, CA 90024
> (213) 555-6782

2. Leave several lines of space, then type CAREER OBJECTIVE at the left side of the paper. Under it, write the goal you'd like to reach, the job you'd really like to have.

3. Leave several lines of space, then type WORK EXPERIENCE at the left side of the paper. List all the jobs you've had, beginning with your most recent job experience and working backwards. Leave one line of space between the entries. Naturally, if you have had only one job, you will report only that one. There are three important items to include in each entry:

    *   the date you started the job and the date you stopped working at the job. (If you still work there, use *present* for the second date.)
    *   your job title and the name and address of your employer. (If you worked for a specific person whom you would like the reader to contact, include his or her name.)
    *   a brief description of your responsibilities.

WORK EXPERIENCE

November 1997–present
Stage Manager
Whoop-De-Doo Productions
1111 Wilship Blvd.
Los Angeles, CA 90024

In charge of all television shows, making sure everything needed for the television sets is ready for the camera operators, supervising the people on the set, working with the directors of the various shows.

July 1995–October 1997
Stagehand
Short Subjects
Dabney Studios
Miller Mall
Los Angeles, CA 90023

Worked for stage manager, gathering props for TV productions, getting sets ready, doing whatever was needed as I learned the business.

4. Leave at least two spaces after this section and type EDUCATION at the left side of your paper. List all the schools you've attended, starting with your most recent educational experience and working back. You don't have to include anything before high school unless you had some unusual educational training. In each entry, include the date you received any degree or diploma from the school, type of degree you obtained, and the name and address of the school. If you attended a school but never received any degree or diploma, write the date you started at the school and the date you left, the same way you wrote the dates for your work experience.

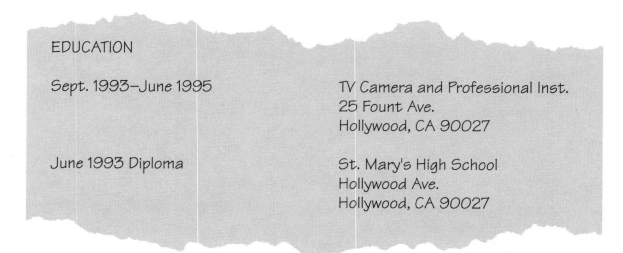

EDUCATION

Sept. 1993–June 1995   TV Camera and Professional Inst.
                             25 Fount Ave.
                             Hollywood, CA 90027

June 1993 Diploma   St. Mary's High School
                             Hollywood Ave.
                             Hollywood, CA 90027

5. If you have received any awards, prizes, or certificates in any of your classes, or if you have participated in any clubs, teams, or other school or community activities, be sure to include them here. They show that you are an active member of your school and community. Type HONORS AND ACTIVITIES at the left side of your paper. Look at how Olga Ortiz listed her honors and activities in the example on page 11.

6. If you have any special skills or training that might help you get the kind of job you're looking for, include those next. Type SKILLS at the left side of your paper, leaving at least two spaces after the previous section. Briefly describe these special skills, just as Olga Ortiz did in her example résumé on page 11.

7. Leave at least two spaces below your last entry and type REFERENCES at the left side of the paper. Then give the names and addresses of two or three people who can provide information about you and your qualifications. The easiest way to list the information is the way you would address an envelope. Be sure to include each person's position or title so the reader can see how these people would know about your abilities.

REFERENCES

Ms. Deborah Leschin, TV Producer
1111 Studio St.
Studio City, CA 91604

Mr. Michael Boggs, Cameraman
4376 Wayne St.
Hollywood, CA 90023

Dr. Jill Johnson, Director
TV Camera and Professional Inst.
25 Fount Ave.
Hollywood, CA 90027

It is very important that a résumé be only one page long. Human Resources employees may read more than fifty résumés for a single job, and they will not have time to read more than one page. Later in your career, you may be listing so many jobs or honors that all your information will not fit on one page. If this is the case, instead of the REFERENCES section, write *References available upon request* at the bottom of your résumé. Then create a second page with the same information on the top as your résumé, and list your references there. Space them out so that they will be attractive and easy to read. You do not need to send your reference page with your résumé. If a potential employer calls to set up an interview, you can offer to fax your references to him or her to help speed up the process. (See *Beginning English Writing Skills*, Chapter 16, Sending a Fax).

There are four golden rules for references:

- Always get permission from people before you use their names. How embarrassing it would be if they are contacted by a potential employer and they say they don't give references, or the employer is unable to get in touch with them because they're sick or out of town, or they've moved.
- Be sure to get the correct spelling of the references' names as well as their correct titles (Director, Chairperson, Instructor, Foreman, etc.).
- Make sure you have the correct address, zip code, and/or telephone number for each reference.
- Don't use a relative as a reference.

8. After you've handwritten a practice copy of your résumé and have checked it for accuracy of names, addresses, dates, and other details, type a practice copy on a typewriter or word processor. Figure out how to space the information so your résumé will be centered on the page, attractive, and easy to read. Type a final copy and proofread it again. Then have several photocopies made so you can apply for as many jobs as you want to without having to retype your résumé each time. You can make your résumé look even more professional by having it typeset and printed on high-quality paper at a print shop.

Practice ▼

Now it's your turn.

Task: to write a résumé

Situation: You want to find a new job, so you need to create a résumé. Write a résumé that will tell potential employers about your work experience, education, and any special skills you have. You will have to use your own paper for this Practice.

3 Job Applications and Résumés

Writing a Cover Letter for a Résumé

Whenever you send a copy of your résumé to a prospective employer, you should send a letter along with it. This cover letter should be brief and specific. It should tell why you are sending your résumé and request the opportunity to be interviewed for a position.

Rationale

If you're interested in a specific job at a specific company, you'll want to send your résumé to that company. Unless you include a letter telling *why* you are sending the résumé, it may never be directed to the proper person or given any attention.

Materials Needed

typewriter or word processor, unlined paper, practice paper, name(s) and address(es) of prospective employers, postage stamp

Skills Involved

using correct letter-writing form; using correct spelling, capitalization, and punctuation; organizing thoughts; typing or word processing neatly

Important Vocabulary

at your convenience at a time that is good for you

autobiography a history of a person's life written by that person

body the main part of a letter; the message

closing a word or phrase used to end a letter. The closing is found just above the writer's signature and is always followed by a comma.

cover letter a letter sent with a résumé to a prospective employer, telling why that person is sending the résumé

indented form a format for writing letters in which the first line of each paragraph is placed farther in from the margin than the salutation. (See page 36 for an example.)

interview a meeting between two or more people. One person is usually at the interview for the purpose of applying for a job or for college. The other person or people are there to ask questions and to decide if the person being interviewed is right for the opening.

look forward to wait for with pleasure

modified block form a format for writing letters in which the margins are the same from the first line to the end. Nothing is indented. A space is left between paragraphs. (See page 36 for an example.)

résumé a list of a person's work and educational experience plus other important background information

return address the address of the person sending a note or letter

salutation the greeting in a letter, usually beginning with *Dear* followed by a person's name or title

Example

400 Lane Drive
Albany, New York 12234
May 28, 19—

Dr. Susan Jones
New York State Education Department
Bureau of Bilingual Education
Albany, New York 12234

Dear Dr. Jones:

Enclosed is my résumé. I am applying for the position of bilingual aide, Spanish/English, as advertised in <u>The Daily Chronicle</u>, May 25, 19—.

I am available for an interview at your convenience and can be reached at 518–555–0202. I look forward to hearing from you.

Sincerely,

Olga Ortiz

Olga Ortiz

Procedure A: Writing the Letter ▼

1. Use unlined paper and make a practice copy first so that your final letter will look professional. Remember, the first impression the reader gets of you will be a visual one.

   a. Type your letter, using single spacing.
   b. Be sure your letter is centered on the page. (It should not be all typed on the top half of the page with a lot of blank white space on the bottom half.)

   By making a practice copy first, you can

   • correct any spelling, punctuation, or capitalization errors,
   • rewrite your sentences to make them as specific as they can be,

- check to see that you have correctly followed either modified block or indented form,
- space your letter so that it is pleasing to the eye.

2. In the upper right corner of the paper, type your address (the *return address*) and the date.

400 Lane Drive
Albany, New York 12234
May 28, 19—

3. Leave a space below the date. Then type the name and address of the person you are writing to on the left side of the paper. This person's name and address should be typed exactly as they will appear on the envelope.

Dr. Susan Jones
New York State Education Department
Bureau of Bilingual Education
Albany, New York 12234

4. Leave a space and then type the salutation.

Dear Dr. Jones:

5. Leave another space and then type the body of your letter. You can use either modified block form or indented form; just don't use a combination of both in the same letter. If you use modified block form, remember to leave a space between paragraphs to show where each new paragraph begins. Your message might look like this:

Enclosed is my résumé. I am applying for the position of bilingual aide, Spanish/English, as advertised in <u>The Daily Chronicle</u>, May 25, 19—.

I am available for an interview at your convenience and can be reached at 518–555–0202. I look forward to hearing from you.

6. Leave a space and then finish your letter by typing *Sincerely* or another appropriate closing on the right. Leave enough space between the closing and your typed name to sign your name in ink.

Sincerely,

Olga Ortiz

Olga Ortiz

7. Read your letter again and correct any errors you find.

8. Sign your name in ink between the closing and your typed name, as shown above.

Practice A ▼

Now it's your turn.

Task: to write a cover letter for your résumé

Situation: You have seen the job you've been waiting for advertised in the local newspaper. You want to send the company your résumé, and you need to write a cover letter to send with it.

The form will look something like this:

_____

_____

_____

_____

_____

_____

_____:

_____

_____

_____

_____

_____

_____,

_____

If the advertisement does not give the name or title of a specific person to write to, you can use *To whom it may concern* or *Dear Sir or Madam* as your salutation. The letter will then be given to the person responsible for reading it.

Procedure B: Addressing the Envelope ▼

The name and address of the person you're writing to should be typed the same way inside the letter and on the envelope.

1. Put your name and address (the *return address*) in the upper left corner of the envelope so that if the letter cannot be delivered for some reason, it will be returned to you.

2. In the center of the envelope, type the name and address of the person you have written to. Put his or her name on the first line. If you don't know the specific name or title, the first line should look exactly as it does in your letter. Next, type the name of the company or organization and its street name and number (if you have this information). The last line of the address should include the city, state, and zip code. If the letter is going outside the country you are writing from, add the name of the country you are sending the letter to and any other necessary information. All the information you need to address the envelope will be given in the advertisement you are answering.

3. Put a postage stamp in the upper right corner. Be sure to use the correct amount of postage, or the letter will not be delivered.

    Your finished envelope might look like this:

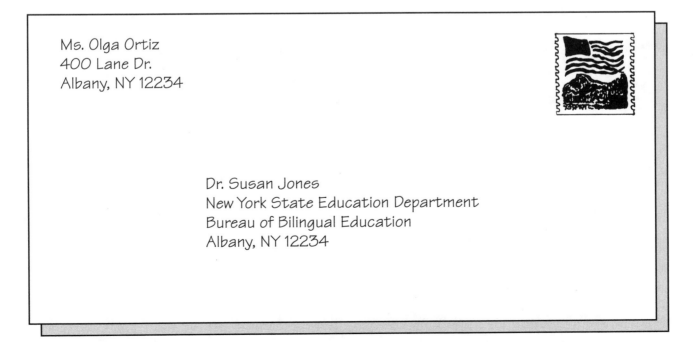

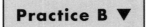

Practice B ▼

Now it's your turn.

Task: to address an envelope

Situation: You have written a cover letter and résumé. Now you want to mail them.

Procedure C: Folding the Letter ▼

1.   If you are using typing paper ($8^{1}/_{2}$" × 11"), fold your paper in thirds. Start by folding the bottom edge up above the middle (a). Then fold the top down, over the bottom fold (b). Use a "business size" envelope.

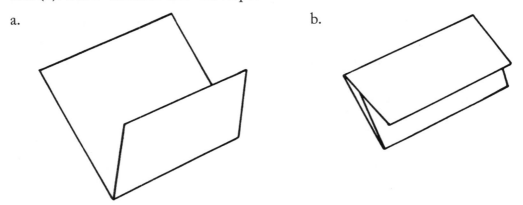

a.   b.

2.   If you have written your letter on smaller stationery, use a matching envelope (one that is appropriate for the size of the stationery). Smaller stationery is usually folded in half:

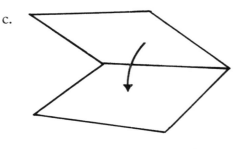

c.

Practice C ▼

Now it's your turn.

Task: to fold your letter properly

Situation: You have proofread your letter, checking your spelling, punctuation, names, and addresses. Your envelope is addressed. Fold your letter and put it in the envelope.

4

Writing a Biodata

There may be a time when potential employers will ask for a Biodata or Curriculum Vitae, which, as the name implies, is a summary of those things that might help them to decide if you are right for the job being offered. Unlike a résumé, which is a listing of your work and educational experience, a biodata or vitae reads like a story of your background. You can include any information that will show something of your abilities, interests, and character. Always start with your present position or most recent accomplishment and work backward, organizing your information in logical order. Try to end with an important statement that will help your biodata or vitae stand out from the rest.

Rationale

People in charge of personnel departments usually ask for vitae from job applicants and then contact the applicants whose vitae show the best qualifications for the type of job involved. If your biodata shows that you have the skills and background that an employer is looking for, and if it's neat and professional in appearance, you may be asked to go in for an interview.

Materials Needed

typewriter or word processor, unlined paper, access to a copying machine, names, addresses, dates of places you've worked and schools you've attended, practice paper, pen or pencil

Skills Involved

organizing material; writing in narrative style; using correct spelling, punctuation, capitalization; typing or word processing

Important Vocabulary

civic relating to the city

designation naming

extensive many

fluent able to communicate easily

preservation saving

Example

BIODATA OF OLGA ORTIZ
400 LANE DR.
ALBANY, NY 12234

Olga Ortiz, Spanish-English bilingual aide, is fluent in three languages: Spanish, English, and French. She has worked with Spanish-speaking arrivals at the Marsh Adult School, 1 Market St., Albany, NY for the past 2 years, helping them to register for English classes and to get adjusted to their new land and language. Olga is a graduate of Passaic County Community College in Paterson, New Jersey, where she was President of the French Club. At Passaic High School, Passaic, New Jersey, she received a Certificate of Merit in Spanish and the Perfect Attendance Award. Olga is involved in many civic activities in Albany, including the preservation and designation as national treasures of historic buildings in the area. Olga has recently completed extensive courses in computer literacy in English and Spanish.

Procedure ▼

1. Make a list of all the information you want to include about yourself. Organize it into work experience, education, and any other important types of information, such as honors or skills, you want to include.

Jobs: baby-sitting, teacher's aide, cashier, volunteer boys' club, math tutor,
Education: City High School, King Community College, President Math Club,
Center basketball team, perfect attendance award
Future: job related to math skills, working with young people

2. Put this information in paragraph form, putting most recent information first. Remember, if you haven't held a paying job yet, include anything you've done while attending school that shows your desire to be productive.

As a sophomore at Martin Luther King Community College, majoring in Math and Economics, Sam Selinger is president of the Math Club and Center on the MLK basketball team. Throughout high school and college he has maintained a perfect attendance record. He worked as a baby-sitter and as a teacher's aide in math classes while attending City High School and also worked after school as a cashier in the Super Saver Supermarket. Once a week during the last two years of high school he worked at the boys' club, tutoring in all phases of math. His goal is to graduate from college, get a degree in education, and become either a high school or college math teacher.

3.   Remember, of course, to include the necessary information for anyone to contact you for an interview. You can include this at the top or bottom of your biodata.

BIODATA
SAM SELINGER
13 David Blvd.
New York, NY 10024
Telephone: 212 222 2222
email: samsel@yes.com

4.   Type your letter in paragraph form as if you were writing a story, using the notes you wrote for yourself in Steps 1 and 2.

BIODATA
SAM SELINGER
13 David Boulevard
New York, New York 10024
Telephone: 212 222 2222
email: samsel@yes.com
Sam Selinger is a sophomore at Martin Luther King Community College, New York, New York, where he is majoring in mathematics and economics. He is President of the Math Club and Center on the Martin Luther King College basketball team. Throughout high school and college he has maintained a perfect attendance record. While attending City High School, Sam worked after school as a baby-sitter and also as a cashier at Super Saver Supermarket to save money for college. Once a week during the last two years of high school he worked as a volunteer at the Boys' Club tutoring students of all ages who were having difficulty in math classes. He also worked as a teacher's aide in math classes in City High School. He plans to obtain his degree in education and to teach math at the high school or college level. Sam would like to continue working in some field of mathematics while completing his education, and is qualified to do so, having already successfully completed courses in advanced trigonometry, calculus, and a minor in economics.

5. You can include the same kind of "cover letter" as you would for a résumé. See "Writing a Cover Letter for a Résumé", page 17.

Now it's your turn.

Task: to write a biodata

Situation: You want to find a part-time job while you are going to school. Write a biodata telling about your schooling so far, including special courses, skills, and training that will help a future employer see something about you and your abilities. Remember to proofread when you're finished!

Unit Two

College Applications

5

Requesting a College Application

At some time in your life, you may decide you want to go to college. Your goal may be to get a degree or just to take some courses. In either case, you will have to fill out a college application. You can get one by writing to the college or university and requesting that an application be sent to you.

Rationale

Different colleges have different entrance requirements, just as different jobs do. Many colleges also specialize in certain subject areas. Therefore, you may need to look at catalogs and applications from several schools to see which ones would be best for you and which ones would be most likely to accept you as a student. The easiest way to obtain the information you need is to write a short letter to the colleges of your choice, requesting an application and a catalog from each one.

Materials Needed

unlined typing paper or stationery, envelopes, postage stamps, pen or typewriter (or word processor)

Skills Involved

organizing thoughts; giving and asking for specific information; using correct punctuation, spelling, capitalization, and abbreviations; typing or handwriting neatly

Important Vocabulary

abbreviation a shortened form of a word; for example, *St.* for *Street*, *NJ* for *New Jersey*

application a form to be completed or filled out requesting admission as a student to a particular school

catalog a book that describes a particular school, giving information on courses offered, how many points (credits) you receive for each course, when the school term begins and ends, and other information about the school

closing a word or phrase used to end a letter. The closing is found just above the writer's signature and is always followed by a comma.

degree a title given by a school to a student who has finished the school's requirements satisfactorily. Degrees most commonly granted by four-year colleges in the United States are the Bachelor of Arts (B.A.) degree and the Bachelor of Science (B.S.) degree.

fill out complete an application (or other form) by writing or typing into spaces all the information that is requested

indented form a format for writing letters in which the first line of each paragraph is placed farther in from the margin than the salutation

legible clear and easy to read

margin the space that is left empty on all four sides of a page containing a letter or other writing

modified block form a format for writing letters in which the margins are the same from the first line to the end. Nothing is indented. A space is left between paragraphs.

requirements those things that are necessary. Some colleges require incoming students to have taken four years of English and three years of science in high school; other colleges require at least two years of a language other than English. A college catalog will list the entrance requirements for that particular college.

return address the address of the person sending a note or letter

salutation the greeting in a letter, usually beginning with *Dear* followed by a person's name

signature a person's name written in his or her own handwriting

Example

top margin	
return address	400 Main St. Brownsville, NH 10231 Sept. 14, 19—
	Director of Admissions Northwestern University Evanston, IL 60204
right margin	
salutation	Dear Sir or Madam:
left margin	I am a junior at Brownsville High School. I expect to graduate in June of 19— and am very interested in attending Northwestern University. Please send me a catalog and an application for admission. Thank you.
closing	Sincerely,
signature	*Kenneth Rinzler*
typed name	Kenneth Rinzler
bottom margin	

Procedure A: Writing the Letter ▼

1.   Once you have decided where you would like to go to college, get the correct address for the school(s) of your choice. If possible, try to get the name of the director of admissions, to make your letter a little more personal. (Most school libraries and high school guidance departments have many books and catalogs containing information that will help you with this step.)

2.   Use unlined stationery. If you have a typewriter or a word processor available, it's always nice to type your letter. Typed letters look more professional and are easier to read. If you are writing your letter by hand, be sure your writing is legible and neat.

3. Leave a margin on all sides of the stationery, and center your letter so it looks good to the eye. If you are typing, use single spacing. Leave a space between
    - the return address and the address of the person you are writing to,
    - the address of the person you are writing to and the salutation,
    - the salutation and the body of the letter, and
    - the body of the letter and the closing.

4. Put your return address in the upper right corner, with your number and street name on the first line; the city, state, and zip code on the second line; and the date on the third line. If you use one abbreviation in the address, use appropriate abbreviations throughout. In other words, if you write Main *St.* instead of Main *Street*, then write Brownsville, *NH* instead of Brownsville, *New Hampshire*. Either style is correct. Never write the date using all numerals, e.g., *9/14/90*. If you have used abbreviations in the address, abbreviate the month: *Sept.* 14, 1990. Otherwise, write out the name of the month.

    Your return address is necessary so the director of admissions will know where to send the catalog and application you are requesting. You don't need to include your name here because that will appear at the bottom of your letter.

    16 Maple St., Apt. 4F
    Portland, OR 97223
    Sept. 12, 19—

5. Leave a space below the date. Then, at the left side of the paper, write the name or title of the person you are writing to and his or her address. Follow the same rules for using abbreviations.

    Ms. Maria Jiménez
    Director of Admissions
    University of Puerto Rico
    Rio Piedras, PR 00924

6.   Leave a space below the address. Then write *Dear* and the name of the person you are writing to. If you don't know the person's name or whether you're addressing a male or female, write *Dear Sir or Madam*. In business letters and other formal letters, the salutation is usually followed by a colon (:) instead of a comma.

> 16 Maple St., Apt. 4F
> Portland, OR 97223
> Sept. 12, 19—
>
> Ms. Maria Jiménez
> Director of Admissions
> University of Puerto Rico
> Rio Piedras, PR 00924
>
> Dear Ms. Jiménez:

7.   Write your message. Be sure to tell the director of admissions what information you would like to receive about the school. Your message might look like one of these:

a. Indented Form

> I plan to graduate from high school in June 19— and would like an application and catalog for the University of Puerto Rico at Rio Piedras. Thank you.

b. Modified Block Form

> I graduated from high school in May 19— and have been working as a data entry clerk since then. Now I would like to take some computer courses at the University of Puerto Rico at Rio Piedras. Please send me a catalog and application and any other information you think would be helpful. Thank you.

8.   Under your message, on the right, end your letter with a word or phrase that shows your appreciation and interest. *Sincerely* is a good closing because it is not too formal and it says that you mean what you wrote. Sign your full name under the closing. If you type your letter, leave enough space to sign your name between the closing and your typed name.

Sincerely,

Alice Quon

Alice Quon

Your finished letter should look something like this:

16 Maple St., Apt. 4F
Portland, OR 97223
Sept. 12, 19—

Ms. Maria Jiménez
Director of Admissions
University of Puerto Rico
Rio Piedras, PR 00924

Dear Ms. Jiménez:

I plan to graduate from high school in June 19— and would like an application and catalog for the University of Puerto Rico at Rio Piedras. Thank you.

Sincerely,

Alice Quon

Alice Quon

Practice A ▼

Now it's your turn. Choose one of the two situations described below.

Task: to write a letter requesting a college application

Situation 1:   You are a junior in high school. You want to know what the specific entrance requirements are for the college of your choice. You write a letter requesting a catalog and an application.

Situation 2:   You are interested in taking courses at a community college (a local two-year college). You would like to know what courses are offered and would like to receive an application.

Remember the form:

_____

_____

_____

_____

_____

_____

_____

_____ :

_____

_____

_____

_____

_____ ,

_____

Procedure B: Addressing the Envelope ▼

The name and address of the person/college you're writing to should be the same inside the letter and on the envelope. If you have typed your letter, the envelope should be typed, too.

1. Put your name and address (the *return address*) in the upper left corner of the envelope so that if the letter cannot be delivered for some reason, it will be returned to you.

2. In the center of the envelope, write or type the name and address of the person you have written to. Put the person's name on one line, the name of the school on the next line, and the city, state, and zip code on the third line. If you know the street name and number, put that information on a separate line right after the name of the school. If the letter is going outside the country you are writing from, be sure to put the name of the country on a line below the city, state, and zip code.

3. Put a postage stamp in the upper right corner. Be sure to use the correct amount of postage, or the letter will not be delivered.

    Your finished envelope might look like this:

Ms. Alice Quon
16 Maple St., Apt. 4F
Portland, OR 97223

Ms. Maria Jiménez, Director of Admissions
University of Puerto Rico
Rio Piedras, PR 00924

Practice B ▼

Now it's your turn.

Task: to address the envelope

Situation: You have written a letter asking for a college application. Now you want to mail it.

Procedure C: Folding the Letter ▼

See the instructions and diagrams for folding a letter on page 24.

Practice C ▼

Now it's your turn.

Task: to fold your letter properly

Situation: You have proofread your letter, checking your spelling, punctuation, names, and addresses. Your envelope is addressed. Fold your letter and put it in the envelope.

Filling Out a College Application

Filling out a college application is an experience you won't soon forget. To do it properly requires time and patience. However, it isn't difficult if you follow the directions and practice on a "dummy" or blank piece of paper first. Rule number one in filling out a college application is DON'T…don't fill it out until you follow the steps shown under Procedure in this chapter.

Rationale

The rationale for filling out a college application is easy: if you want to go to college, the first thing you must do is fill out the college application correctly.

Materials Needed

pencils, pen, typewriter or word processor if application must be typed, scrap paper, application, envelope, appropriate postage, information required by college (for example, parents' financial aid statement), check or money order for any application fee(s)

Skills Involved

reading comprehension; paying attention to details, spelling, grammar, and punctuation; outlining; selecting and organizing appropriate material for writing a coherent essay; essay writing; meeting deadlines; following directions; using neat, legible handwriting; typing (if required)

Important Vocabulary

admissions committee or **admissions board** the group of people who read your application and decide if you should be admitted to a school

application fee money that must be sent (by check or money order, never cash) with your application for admission to some colleges

assets things that have monetary value, such as a house, a car, or a savings account

brochure a small printed booklet

campus the grounds and buildings of a college or university

candidate someone who is applying for a position

class rank a number assigned to a student to indicate his or her position among all the students at that grade level. Class rank is determined by comparing each student's course grades to the grades of the other class members.

credentials written proof of abilities, qualifications, and suitability for a position

deposit an amount of money that must be sent to a school (once you have been accepted) to indicate that you plan to attend that school. The deposit holds your place in the school and is usually *nonrefundable*, which means you will not get the money back if you decide later not to go to that school.

dormitory a college-owned building with living quarters for students. Dormitories usually contain bedrooms, bathrooms, communal living rooms, and sometimes a dining area.

essay a relatively short piece of writing that expresses the writer's feelings or opinions on a certain subject

family income the amount of money a family earns in a year

fee waiver a decision to allow someone not to pay a normally required fee (amount of money)

financial aid money (usually in the form of loans, scholarships, and/or paid jobs on campus) provided to a student to help pay for his or her college education

forfeit lose; give up

foster parents persons (not biological parents) who are in charge of a child's financial support and well-being

freshman a first-year student in high school or college

funds money

guardian a person who is legally responsible for another person

interview a meeting between an applicant for a school or job and the person(s) who will decide if the applicant is right for the school or job. See "Requesting an Interview," pages 71–80.

outline an organized list of the main ideas to be expressed in an essay

proofread read for the purpose of finding and correcting any errors

reservation a guarantee that a place has been saved for someone

scrap paper extra paper; paper that is not intended for a specific purpose

submit send in or present

transcript a record of a student's marks or grades at a particular school

transfer student a student who has attended one school and changes to another school before completing the requirements for a degree

waiting list a list of people who are in line to be admitted by a school. If a place at the school becomes available, the next person on the waiting list will be admitted.

Example

See next page.

Northwestern

Application for Freshman Admission

1998–99

NORTHWESTERN UNIVERSITY *Instructions*

Before You Start

This booklet contains the following materials:

- **Application for Freshman Admission Part 1** (two sides: pages 5–6)
- **Application for Freshman Admission Part 2** (four-page booklet: pages 7–10)
- **Secondary School Report** (two sides: pages 11–12)
- **Midyear School Report** (two sides: pages 13–14)
- **Teacher Recommendation** (two sides: pages 15–16)
- **Acknowledgment card** (stapled in center)
- **Honors Program in Medical Education request card** (stapled in center; see page 3)
- **Return envelope** (enclosed)

Fill out Parts 1 and 2 and the acknowledgment card and return them to Northwestern University by the application deadline. Fill out the appropriate portions of the Secondary School Report, Midyear School Report (regular decision applicants only), and Teacher Recommendation and give them to the appropriate person(s) at your secondary school to complete and submit to Northwestern by the appropriate deadline.

1. Applying to Northwestern

The Office of Undergraduate Admission must receive all application materials by the appropriate deadline. Northwestern University will not return any materials submitted for admission consideration. In addition to the materials included in this booklet, you must submit the following to be considered for admission.

Nonrefundable Application Fee or Fee Waiver

Write your name and Social Security number on a $55 check payable to Northwestern University and submit it with Part 1 of this application. If you are a U.S. citizen or permanent resident, your family income is less than $20,000 a year, and your family has limited assets, you may request a fee waiver by attaching a letter signed by you and your parents that states these conditions.

Required Standardized Test Results

All applicants must also submit the results of either the Scholastic Assessment Test (SAT I) or the American College Test (ACT). You should take these tests before your application deadline and request that the testing agency send your results directly to Northwestern. The Northwestern SAT I code is 1565; the ACT code is 1106.

In addition, you may be required to submit other test results.

TOEFL Results If your native language is not English, you also must present the results of the Test of English as a Foreign Language (TOEFL). For more information, write to the Office of Undergraduate Admission and request the international student brochure.

SAT II Results Applicants to the Honors Program in Medical Education and the Integrated Science Program are required to submit the results of three SAT IIs (see page 3). Although not required, we recommend that all applicants take three SAT IIs before the admission deadline. Request that your scores be sent to Northwestern.

EARLY DECISION DEADLINES AND CHECKLIST

Due by	Required item
As soon as possible (no later than November 1)	☐ Part 1 and the $55 fee ☐ Acknowledgment card
October testing date	☐ All required tests (see instruction 1)
November 1	☐ Part 2 ☐ Secondary School Report ☐ Teacher Recommendation
November 15	☐ Music applicants: schedule audition
December 15	Northwestern admission decision
February 1	☐ Applicants' reply/$200 deposit
March 15	☐ Room reservation/$200 deposit

FINANCIAL AID DEADLINES AND CHECKLIST

Due by	Required item
November 1	☐ CSS Financial Aid Profile registration (see instruction 3)
December 1	☐ CSS Financial Aid Profile application (see instruction 3)
February 1	☐ FAFSA (see instruction 3)

REGULAR DECISION DEADLINES AND CHECKLIST

Due by	Required item
As soon as possible (no later than January 1)	☐ Part 1 and the $55 fee ☐ Acknowledgment card
December testing date	☐ All required tests (see instruction 1)
January 1	☐ Part 2 ☐ Secondary School Report ☐ Teacher Recommendation
February 1	☐ Music applicants: schedule audition
Mid-February	☐ Midyear School Report
April 15	Northwestern admission decision
May 1	☐ Applicants' reply/$200 deposit
May 25	☐ Room reservation/$200 deposit

FINANCIAL AID DEADLINES AND CHECKLIST

Due by	Required item
January 1	☐ CSS Financial Aid Profile registration (see instruction 3)
February 1	☐ CSS Financial Aid Profile application (see instruction 3)
February 1	☐ FAFSA (see instruction 3)

N O R T H W E S T E R N   U N I V E R S I T Y *Instructions*

Home Schooling Applicants who have been educated at home are required to submit the results of three SAT II exams in addition to SAT I or ACT results. (Results from SAT II Writing, SAT II Mathematics Level IIC, and a third test of your choice are required.)

RECOMMENDED SAT IIs

If you apply to . . .	Take . . .
College of Arts and Sciences, Medill School of Journalism, Schools of Education and Social Policy, Music, and Speech	Writing plus two others
McCormick School of Engineering and Applied Science	Mathematics I or IIC, Chemistry or Physics, and Writing

---

School of Music Applicants: Audition
All School of Music applicants must schedule an audition before February 1 (before November 15 for Early Decision applicants). For more information, contact the School of Music at 847/491-3141.

2. Application Deadlines
When you apply for fall quarter admission to Northwestern as a freshman, you may choose Early Decision or Regular Decision.

Early Decision
If Northwestern is your clear first choice, the Early Decision option will ensure that you have an admission decision before the application deadline for many other schools. Because Early Decision is binding, you may not apply to other colleges under their binding plans. If you are accepted to Northwestern under Early Decision, you must withdraw all other university applications. Unlike other highly selective schools, Northwestern does not make a practice of deferring Early Decision applicants into our Regular Decision pool. If you are denied admission to Northwestern under Early Decision, you may not reapply under Regular Decision.

Change from Early to Regular Decision
To change from Early Decision to Regular Decision, you must request the change before December 1. If we have already mailed your admission decision under Early Decision, you cannot apply under Regular Decision and your reply deadline will not be changed.

Winter or Spring Quarter Freshmen
Freshmen wishing to enter Northwestern for winter or spring quarter must submit all required materials by November 1 or February 1, respectively, of the academic year in which they plan to attend. Applicants from other countries must apply for fall quarter entrance.

3. Financial Aid Applicants
Northwestern awards financial aid on the basis of need, using federal, state, and institutional guidelines. Detailed financial aid information is available from the Office of Undergraduate Admission.

How to Apply
Do not wait until you have been admitted to Northwestern or have filed federal income tax forms to apply for financial aid. If you fail to meet the financial aid deadline, notification of your award will be delayed or funds may be entirely committed.

a) Notify Northwestern Check "Yes" in item 11, Part 1, of the Application for Freshman Admission.

b) File the College Scholarship Service (CSS) Profile Application Register with CSS before January 1 (before November 1 for Early Decision applicants) by calling 1-800-778-6888 (http://www.collegeboard.org/). Indicate Northwestern's Financial Aid Profile code (1565). CSS will send you a customized Profile application. Complete and return the Profile application to CSS no later than February 1 (December 1 for Early Decision applicants).

c) File the Free Application for Federal Student Aid (FAFSA) Obtain the FAFSA from your secondary school counselor or call 1-800-4FED-AID (http://www.ed.gov/offices/OPE/). Complete the FAFSA and mail it to the federal processor by February 1 (but not before January 1). Request that your aid analysis be forwarded to Northwestern (FAFSA code 001739).

Winter and Spring Quarter Applicants
Freshmen applying for a quarter other than fall must submit the FAFSA and the CSS Financial Aid Profile application at least one month before their admission deadline.

Foreign Applicants
Foreign nationals must be permanent residents of the United States to be eligible for financial aid from Northwestern. Financial aid applicants who are not U. S. citizens are asked to submit proof of permanent resident status.

Special Aid Consideration
Business/Farm Owners By the filing deadline, owners of businesses and/or farms should submit the Business/Farm Supplement directly to Northwestern. The supplement should be included in your CSS Financial Aid Profile application packet.

Divorced or Separated Parents If your parents are separated or divorced, the custodial parent must file the FAFSA and CSS Financial Aid Profile application. By the filing deadline, the noncustodial parent must submit directly to Northwestern the Divorced/Separated Parents Statement, which should be included in your CSS Financial Aid Profile application packet.

Illinois Residents If you live in Illinois, you may apply for the Monetary Grant awarded by the Illinois Student Assistance Commission (ISAC) by completing the FAFSA, including the state-specific information.

National Merit/National Achievement Scholarships Qualified National Merit or National Achievement scholarship candidates must indicate to the National Merit Scholarship Corporation that Northwestern is their first choice. You must also apply for financial aid and demonstrate need.

Reserve Officer Training Corps Naval, Air Force, or Army ROTC applicants should apply for financial aid if they believe that their family cannot afford the cost of a Northwestern education without a military scholarship.

NORTHWESTERN UNIVERSITY *Special Admission Programs*

Engineering Honors Programs

Honors Program in Engineering and Education This joint program between the McCormick School of Engineering and Applied Science and the School of Education and Social Policy is designed for students who believe that an engineering background will give them an advantage in enhancing human learning through the development of new educational or training materials. If accepted into this program, you will complete a bachelor's degree in engineering and a master's degree in the learning sciences in five years.

Honors Program in Engineering and Journalism If you have a strong interest in engineering and the desire to develop effective communication skills, this program allows you to complete a bachelor's degree in the McCormick School and a master's degree in the Medill School of Journalism in five years.

Honors Program in Engineering and Management If you have an interest in the management of engineering and technology, this program offers you undergraduate engineering course work interspersed with 6 quarters of cooperative education work experience and deferred admission to the J. L. Kellogg Graduate School of Management.

Honors Program in Undergraduate Research This honors program, offered through the McCormick School, provides you with the opportunity to work with an engineering faculty adviser in developing your own research project as early as your freshman year. With Advanced Placement credit and satisfactory performance, you may be considered during your junior year for admission to the Graduate School for accelerated progress toward a PhD.

How to Apply

To qualify for admission consideration for the above honors programs you must:

a) Write the McCormick School before December 1 To receive the special honors program application and additional information, contact the McCormick School of Engineering and Applied Science, Northwestern University, Evanston, Illinois 60208-3102, e-mail mccormick-school@nwu.edu. (Indicate which honors program you are interested in.)

b) Submit the Special Honors Program Application Applicants must submit the special honors program application by January 15.

c) Submit the Application for Admission You must select a major in the McCormick School of Engineering and Applied Science (item 8, Part 1).

Honors Program in Medical Education

The Honors Program in Medical Education (HPME) is a seven-year program leading to an MD degree. To be selected for HPME consideration, complete both sides of the HPME application request card (stapled in the center of this booklet) and return it to the Office of Undergraduate Admission by December 1. Only qualified applicants are sent HPME applications.

HPME applicants must apply under Regular Decision by January 1. When filling in a proposed major in item 8, Part 1, select any major (or undecided) in the College of Arts and

DEADLINES FOR THE HONORS PROGRAM IN MEDICAL EDUCATION	
HPME request card*	December 1
Required tests†	December test date
HPME application	January 1
Application for admission	January 1

* The request card can be found stapled in the center of this booklet
† ACT or SAT I and SAT II (results are required in Chemistry, Mathematics Level IIC, and Writing)

DEADLINES FOR THE INTEGRATED SCIENCE PROGRAM AND MATHEMATICAL METHODS IN THE SOCIAL SCIENCES		
ISP and MMSS applications may be filed later than your application for admission. To ensure a timely decision, apply by the following deadlines.		
	Early Decision	*Regular Decision*
Application for admission	November 1	January 1
Program application	January 1	March 1
Required tests*	December test date	January test date

* ACT or SAT I. ISP applicants must also submit three SAT II results: Chemistry or Physics, Mathematics Level IIC, and a second science. If the Writing test is required for another application, the second science can be waived for ISP.

Sciences; or indicate biomedical engineering as your major in the McCormick School of Engineering and Applied Science; or indicate communication sciences and disorders in the School of Speech.

SAT II Results HPME applicants must take the Chemistry, Mathematics IIC, and Writing SAT IIs (no substitutions are allowed) by the December test date; request that the scores be sent to Northwestern University (code 1565).

Integrated Science Program

The Integrated Science Program (ISP) is an accelerated program providing interdisciplinary study in the natural sciences. To receive an application for ISP, check the appropriate box in item 10, Part 1. You must submit the ISP application by January 1 for Early Decision or March 1 for Regular Decision. When filling in a proposed major in item 8, Part 1, you must also select a major (or undecided) in the College of Arts and Sciences.

For additional information, write to Director, Integrated Science Program, Northwestern University, Evanston, Illinois 60208-4160, e-mail info@isp.nwu.edu.

Mathematical Methods in the Social Sciences

Mathematical Methods in the Social Sciences (MMSS) is an accelerated program that integrates the study of mathematics, statistics, and computers with the social sciences. To receive an application to the MMSS program, check the appropriate box in item 10, Part 1. When filling in a proposed major in item 8, Part 1, you must also select a major (or undecided) in the College of Arts and Sciences.

For additional information, write to Director, Mathematical Methods in the Social Sciences, Northwestern University, Evanston, Illinois 60208-2250, e-mail mmss@nwu.edu.

NORTHWESTERN UNIVERSITY *Application for Freshman Admission*

PART I

You must submit Part I to become a formal applicant to Northwestern University.

Application Status

1. Foreign students must apply for fall quarter.

Freshman applicant, fall
☐ Early Decision: Deadline, November 1
■ Regular Decision: Deadline, January 1

Freshman applicant, other quarter
☐ Winter: Deadline, November 1
☐ Spring: Deadline, February 1

Office Use

2. Have you previously applied for admission?   ☐ Yes/year _____   ■ No
Do you have a course catalog?   ☐ Yes   ■ No

Personal Information

Return Part I and the nonrefundable $55 application fee (put your name and Social Security number on the check, payable to Northwestern University) in the envelope provided as soon as possible but no later than your application deadline.

3. Full legal name   *Kohn*   *Tova*
   last (family)   first   middle

Other names you have used   ——————
   last (family)   first   middle

Social Security number *123-45-6789*   Date of birth *12 / 15 / 80*   Sex ■ Female ☐ Male
                                              month day year

4. Permanent address   *1410 Abbot St.*
   number, street, apt. no.

Lincolnwood   *IL*   *60646*   *USA*
city   state   zip   country

Phone *847 - 555-1279*   E-mail address ———   Fax ———
   area code   number   area code   number

5. Current mailing address   *Same as above*
   number, street, apt. no.

city   state   zip   country

Phone   Current mailing address effective until what date? _/_/_
   area code   number   month day year

6. Are you a U.S. citizen? ☐ (1) Yes ■ No Country of citizenship *Cuba*
   If you are *not* a U.S. citizen, are you a permanent resident of the United States? ■ (3) Yes ☐ (2) No
   If you are living in the United States and are *not* a permanent resident, what is your visa classification? _____

7. How would you describe yourself? (optional)
   ☐ (1) Alaskan native/Native American
   ☐ (3) Asian/Pacific islander (including Indian subcontinent)
   ☐ (2) Black/African American, not of Hispanic origin
   ☐ (6) Caucasian/White, not of Hispanic origin
   ☐ (4) Hispanic, not Mexican American or Puerto Rican
   ☐ (7) Mexican American/Chicano
   ☐ (8) Puerto Rican
   ☐ (9) Other _____

Academic Interests

8. Proposed major (choose one; see page 4): three-digit code *053*   and name of major *Business*

School of Music applicants must audition; see instruction 1.

9. Performance area (School of Music applicants only; see page 4): two-digit code _____ and name of area _____
   To apply to a School of Music five-year double-degree program, check the appropriate box:
   ☐ (598) Music and engineering
   ☐ (597) Music and liberal arts

ISP and MMSS require an additional application; see page 3.

10. If you want to apply to one of the following programs (see "Special Admission Programs" on page 3), indicate a major (or undecided) in the College of Arts and Sciences in item 8 and check the appropriate box below.
   ☐ Integrated Science Program
   ☐ Mathematical Methods in the Social Sciences

Financial aid is available only to U.S. citizens and permanent residents.

Request for Financial Aid Consideration

11. Are you seeking financial aid from Northwestern?   ■ Yes   ☐ No
   Do you intend to apply for the following scholarships?   ☐ NROTC   ☐ AFROTC   ☐ AROTC
   ☐ Evans (Western Golf Association)

(over)

NORTHWESTERN UNIVERSITY *Application for Freshman Admission*

PART I

School Information

12. List all secondary schools you have attended (if more than one, list the most recent below and the remainder on a separate sheet)

Name of school   Lincolnwood High School   Lincolnwood   IL
                                           city   state

Six-digit CEEB code   000234   Dates attended   9/94   6/98
                                                from   to

Family Information

13. Relative(s) who are employed by Northwestern   ☐ Father   ☐ Mother   ☐ Sibling   ☐ Outside immediate family

Name, relationship, and position

14. Relative(s) who are attending/have attended Northwestern   ☐ Father   ☐ Mother   ☐ Sibling   ☐ Outside immediate family

Name, relationship, dates, and school of attendance

15. Father's name   Kohn   Abraham   Mother's name   Kohn   Ruth   L.
                    last   first   initial   last   first   initial

Home phone   847   555 - 1279   Home phone   847 - 555 - 1279
             area code   number   area code   number

Work phone   630   554 - 0000   Work phone   847 - 555 - 1449
             area code   number   area code   number

Statement of Academic Integrity

Northwestern students and faculty are committed to scholarly principles that respect and acknowledge individual achievement. Because of this, certain behaviors are viewed as unacceptable, including cheating, plagiarism, falsifying or fabricating information, and aiding and abetting academic dishonesty. Students who violate these principles are subject to penalties, including course failure and dismissal from Northwestern.

You must sign this statement. The Office of Undergraduate Admission reviews only applications that have been signed.

All Applicants

I certify that to the best of my knowledge all statements by me are correct, complete, and my own. If admitted to Northwestern University, I will abide by the standards of academic integrity expected of Northwestern students. I understand that this application and all other records gathered for my admission files are confidential and will not be disclosed to me or any other person, except as provided by law. I understand that the knowing submission of false or misleading information may, in Northwestern's sole discretion, result in denial or revocation of admission.

Applicant's signature   *Tova Kohn*   Date   11/15/97

If you are applying under Early Decision, you, your parent, and your secondary school counselor must also sign this statement.

Early Decision Applicants

I have read and understand the conditions of the Early Decision option. By applying under Early Decision, I hereby indicate that Northwestern is my first-choice college and the only college to which I have applied under an early decision plan. If offered admission, I will accept Northwestern's offer, withdraw all other applications, and initiate no new applications. (All three signatures are required.)

Return to the Office of Undergraduate Admission, P.O. Box 3060, Evanston, Illinois 60204-3060.

Early Decision applicant's signature   Date

Parent/guardian's signature

Secondary school adviser/counselor's signature

6

NORTHWESTERN UNIVERSITY *Application for Freshman Admission*

PART 2

Return Part 2 as soon as possible but no later than your application deadline.

Part 2 is a four-page booklet; do not tear at the fold.

Name   **Kohn**   **Tova**   Social Security number **123-45-6789**
     last   first   middle

Date of birth **12/15/80**   Place of birth **Tierra Del Fuego**   **Cuba**
     month day year   city   state/province   country

1. Foreign citizens residing in the United States: How long have you lived in the United States? **8 years**

2. Is a language other than English spoken at home? ■ Yes ☐ No   If yes, what language? **Spanish**

Housing

3. Where do you plan to live while attending Northwestern? ☐ University housing ■ At home ☐ Off campus

Family Information

List stepparents in item 5.

4. Father's name **Kohn**   **Abraham**   Mother's name **Kohn**   **Ruth**   **L.**
    last   first   initial   last   first   initial

Address   Address
    if different from your permanent address: number, street, apt. no.   if different from your permanent address: number, street, apt. no.

city   state   zip   country   city   state   zip   country

Employer **Whistler's Restaurant**   Employer **Oak Brook Mfg.**
    if self-employed, state nature of business   if self-employed, state nature of business

Position **Waiter**   Position **factory worker**

Place of birth **Havana, Cuba**   Place of birth **Havana, Cuba**

Secondary school attended **Colegio Superior**   Secondary school attended **Colegio Superior**

College(s) attended   College(s) attended
    name   no. of years   degree   name   no. of years   degree

Universidad Nacional   **4**   **BS**
    name   no. of years   degree   name   no. of years   degree

If deceased, give date   If deceased, give date

5. Do you have ☐ foster parents ☐ a guardian ☐ stepparents? If so, please give name(s) and address(es).

Name   Name
    last   first   initial   last   first   initial

Address   Address
    number, street, apt. no.   number, street, apt. no.

city   state   zip   country   city   state   zip   country

Phone   Phone
    area code   number   area code   number

6. In case of emergency, who should be Northwestern's initial contact?
☐ Father ■ Mother ☐ Guardian ☐ Other

7. Number of siblings: older ____, younger **3**, twin ____. Is a sibling also applying to Northwestern this year? ☐ Yes ■ No
How many of your siblings have attended or are attending college? **0**

Educational Information

8. Are you interested in participating in intercollegiate debate? ■ Yes ☐ No

9. Indicate if you are considering one or more of the following for graduate study:
■ Business/management ☐ Dentistry ☐ Law ■ Medicine

(over)

7

N O R T H W E S T E R N   U N I V E R S I T Y   *Application for Freshman Admission*

PART 2

10. Please indicate the number of courses (year course = 1, semester course = ½) that you are taking or have taken during secondary school (grades 9–12) in the following academic areas. If applicable, also indicate the number of courses that were accelerated (ACC) and honors (H) or Advanced Placement (AP) and International Baccalaureate (IB).

Subject	Total Number	ACC/H	AP/IB	Subject	Total Number	ACC/H	AP/IB
English	4	1		Laboratory science	4	1	
Foreign language	4			Mathematics	3		
History/social science	4	1		Electives	5		

11. List all senior-year courses, identifying any that are Advanced Placement (AP), honors (H), accelerated (ACC), or International Baccalaureate (IB). List college courses taken during secondary school and the institution where the courses were taken.

First semester/trimester	Second semester/trimester	Third trimester
English Literature	Same	
French IV		
World History		
Calculus		
Advanced Biology		

12. List the scores you received on the following tests and the dates they were taken. Indicate any future test dates.

Test	Score	Date	Test	Score	Date
SAT I Verbal	590	10/1/97	SAT II		
			subject		
SAT I Math	670	10/1/97			
			subject		
AP:					
subject			subject		
			ACT Composite	29	3/26/97
subject					

13. Applicants whose native language is not English: How long have you attended schools where you were instructed in English? __8 years__ TOEFL score __640__ Date __8/15/97__

14. Have you ever been suspended or dismissed from secondary school? ☐ Yes ■ No
If yes, please explain fully on a separate sheet.

General Information

15. Have you visited the Northwestern campus? ■ Yes. When? __Several times__ ☐ No
Have you met or do you plan to meet with a Northwestern alumni admission representative?
☐ Yes. Where? _____ When? _____ ■ No

16. Which of the following encouraged your interest in Northwestern University? You may check more than one.

☐ Northwestern hotel program. Where? _____ When? _____

☐ College fair/high school visit by Northwestern representative. Where? _____ When? _____

■ Teacher, friend, or family member. Who? __Linda Schinke__ Relationship? __Teacher__

■ Northwestern student or graduate, not a family member. Who? __Becky Rauff__

■ Information about Northwestern ■ Sent at my request ☐ From another source What? _____

8

(do not detach; continue on page 9)

NORTHWESTERN UNIVERSITY *Application for Freshman Admission*

PART 2

Name _Kohn_ _Tova_
last   first   middle

Date of birth _12_ / _15_ / _80_   Social Security number _123-45-6789_
month day year

Honors and Awards

List any distinctions or honors you have earned since ninth grade.

	School year 9 10 11 12
National Merit Finalist	▢ ▢ ▢ ■

Activity Chart

List your four most important time commitments other than academic work during the last several years (for example: school organizations, jobs, religious groups, the arts, service, athletics, individual interests).

Activity (in order of importance to you)	School year 9 10 11 12	Approximate time involved: hours per week/ weeks per year	Positions held, honors won, or letters earned
Part-time Job	■■	12/52	Assistant to Mgr.
Nursing Home Visits	■■	2/40	Volunteer
French Club	■■	1/10	Secretary
Student Council	■	2/40	Class Representative

Additional time commitments other than academic work

School-related

		/	
		/	
		/	
		/	
		/	
		/	
		/	
		/	
		/	
		/	
		/	

Nonschool-related (including interests, hobbies, and jobs)

		/	
		/	
		/	
		/	
		/	

Summer activities (not including jobs)

		/	
		/	
		/	

(over)

9

PART 2

Personal Statements

Please respond to one of the essay topics below. Please note which topic you are addressing at the beginning of your essay. Your essay must be typed (from 400 to 500 words) and submitted on separate sheets of paper. Type your name and Social Security number on each sheet, and staple all the sheets to this page.

Essay Topics

- What effect has any voluntary or independent research, reading or study, work in the arts, science project, etc., had on your intellectual and personal growth in recent years? Discuss what influence this involvement has had on your academic goals.
- History has recorded the American Revolution, the Industrial Revolution, and the Sexual Revolution. Today we are witnessing a revolution in the way we receive information. What do you think will be the next great revolution, and what will be its impact on you and society?
- George Washington said, "Associate with men of good quality, if you esteem your own reputation; it is better to be alone than in bad company." About which of your friends do you and your parents disagree? Why do you feel that the continued company of this friend is a good thing?
- Imagine you have written a short story, film, or play about your last four years. Briefly describe the moment or scene that you think your audience will most remember after they have finished this autobiographical piece. What will they learn about you from that moment?

Applicants not in school: Attach to the essay you have written an explanation of why you discontinued your studies. What have you been doing since leaving school?

Northwestern Statement

What are your reasons for wanting to attend Northwestern? (You may use a separate sheet of paper to answer this question.)

I want to spend my college years close to home, studying thought-provoking subjects with diverse people, and participating in a variety of activities. All these experiences will help me find out what I'm good at, and what I really enjoy. Then I'll be able to choose the career that's best for me, and pull my life together into a promising future.

Short Statements

Please respond to the following questions in the space provided.

What creative work (outside your school curriculum) has influenced your way of thinking?

Volunteering in a nursing home has made me more sensitive to the needs of others. It is so important for us to give of ourselves.

What high school course do you wish you had taken and why?

I wish I had taken Auto Mechanics, because I probably won't get another chance to take a course like that, and it's very practical.

The Northwestern students recently voted to increase their activity fees in order to bring more speakers and groups to campus. What speaker or group would you most want to see?

I would like to see someone like Jaime Escalante, who has succeeded in spite of obstacles.

Northwestern's most unusual tradition is the painting of a stone monstrosity known as "the Rock." Students take turns painting it with slogans promoting political views, advertising campus activities, or expressing personal feelings. If given the opportunity, what message would you paint on the Rock?

LOVE is a four-letter word.

Return to the Office of Undergraduate Admission, P.O. Box 3060, Evanston, Illinois 60204-3060.

Procedure ▼

1. If possible, make a copy of the application and use the copy to practice writing your answers. Or, answer all the questions on scrap paper first. Do not write on the original application yet.

2. Read *all* the directions on the application carefully. Ask a guidance counselor, teacher, parent, or anyone else who can help you about anything you don't understand. It is never wrong to say that you don't understand something, even if you think it is probably something very simple.

3. Pay particular attention to directions that tell whether the application must be typed or printed in your own handwriting.

4. Read the directions a second time, following them one by one on your practice copy or scrap paper.

5. After you have practiced answering all the informational questions, print or type your answers on the actual application, making sure to follow directions such as "Last name first." Proofread as you go along. If you're typing, make sure that you have hit the letters you meant to hit and that you are working in the right spaces.

6. Before you begin writing the answer to an essay question, make an outline on scrap paper. (See "Making an Outline," pages 82–92.) Check your outline to be sure that it includes all the information you want and that the information is in the proper sequence.

7. Write your essay on scrap paper, following your outline. See Chapter 10, "Writing an Essay," for an example.

8. Proofread your essay. Make corrections, additions, and/or deletions. Check your spelling, grammar, and punctuation. If possible, ask a teacher or guidance counselor to read your essay before you print or type it on the application form.

9. Type or print your essay(s) on the application.

10. The next day, proofread your application one more time.

11. If possible, have a parent, teacher, or counselor look over your application before you mail it. Be sure you attach any other forms and/or checks that are required.

Now it's your turn.

Task: to fill out a college application

Situation: You want to apply to a college. You have received the application and must now complete it. Remember:

- read all the directions first,

- use scrap paper to practice your answers before you even write your name on the actual application,

- consult the chapter on "Making an Outline" (pages 82–92) for help with your essay answers, and

- proofread everything carefully when you're finished.

APPLICATION FOR
UNDERGRADUATE ADMISSION

WILLIAM PATERSON UNIVERSITY

HELPING TO MAKE YOUR LIFE WORK

APPLICATION INFORMATION AND INSTRUCTIONS

INFORMATION AND INSTRUCTIONS
- ALL APPLICANTS
- APPLICATION DEADLINES
- PROOF OF HIGH SCHOOL GRADUATION
- ART AND MUSIC MAJORS
- FRESHMAN STUDENTS
- ADVANCED STANDING STUDENTS
- SPECIAL ADMISSION
- ADVANCED PLACEMENT
- VETERANS
- SCHOLARSHIPS AND FINANCIAL AID
- APPLICATION FORM
- EDUCATIONAL OPPORTUNITY FUND (EOF)

ALL APPLICANTS
Priority Service
Because the number of applications has continued to increase over the past several years, William Paterson College has experienced unprecedented demand for services to new students. It is now essential that students interested in attending William Paterson College apply for admission and related services (financial aid, scholarships, residence hall space and testing) as early as possible. To encourage early applications, William Paterson College has instituted the Priority Service Program.

In the Priority Service Program, students accepted to the College by April 1 for fall admission and by October 1 for spring admission will receive priority service from participating offices. While April 1 and October 1 are the priority service deadlines, students may apply much earlier, and they are encouraged to do so.

APPLICATION DEADLINES
Application and supporting official transcripts for freshmen, transfer, second-degree and re-admit students must be received by the deadline dates shown below:

Fall – May 1   Spring – November 1

NOTE: In order to maintain quality programs and student services, the College will adhere to the printed deadlines. Failure to submit complete official records of all prior college coursework and high school transcripts, when required, will result in a delay in the application review process.

VOICE RESPONSE SERVICE
Priority service through individualized appointments and course registration is provided for advanced standing students accepted by April 1 for the spring semester and October 1 for the fall semester.

PROOF OF HIGH SCHOOL GRADUATION
In order to comply with state and federal regulations regarding immunization and financial aid, all applicants (freshmen, transfer, second baccalaureate and re-admit students) MUST submit proof of high school graduation (copy of high school diploma or high school transcripts with date of graduation posted). All students who have graduated from high school or who have earned a GED must submit additional paperwork from their physician to satisfy proof of immunization. Students will not be allowed to register without compliance with applicable state and federal regualtions.

ART AND MUSIC MAJORS
All freshman, transfer and second baccalaureate degree students selecting art as their major must submit a portfolio for review by the Art Department as part of the admissions criteria. Information regarding the review will be sent to you upon receipt of your application, or you may contact the Art Department at (201) 595-2404.

All freshmen, transfer and second baccalaureate degree students selecting music as their major must audition as part of the admissions criteria. Information regarding the audition will be sent to you upon receipt of your application, or you may contact the Music Department at (201) 595-2315. In addition to passing the portfolio review or audition, students must meet regular admission criteria as well. Passing the departmental requirements does not automatically admit one to the College.

FRESHMAN STUDENTS
Admission Requirements
Freshman candidates are required to have an official high school transcript and SAT or ACT scores sent to the Office of Admissions.

High School Record
Admissions criteria include having taken a minimum of sixteen (16) Carnegie Units and having demonstrated good academic ability. Your record must show the following courses:

Subject Area	Minimum Unit Requirements	
English	4	Composition
		Literature
Mathematics	3	Algebra I
		Geometry
		Algebra II
Laboratory	2	Biology
		Chemistry
		Physics

Laboratory science requirements may be chosen from biology, chemistry, physics, earth sciences or anatomy/physiology.

Social Science	2	American History
		World History
		Political Science
Additional College Preparatory Subjects	5	Advanced Math
		Literature
		Foreign Language
		Social Sciences

Certain departments have specific requirements beyond those listed above.
- Students who plan to major in mathematics or science are expected to have taken more than the minimum courses in those areas.
- Nursing students need a full year of both biology and chemistry.
- GED – A high school equivalency diploma recognized by New Jersey may be presented in place of the above requirements.

SAT/ACT REQUIREMENTS
Entering freshmen students must have taken the Scholastic Aptitude Test (SAT) or the American College Test (ACT) and have their scores sent to the Office of Admissions, William Paterson College. To submit your scores to WPC, indicate code 2518 for the SAT and code 2584 for the ACT.

ADVANCED STANDING STUDENTS
(Transfer, Second Baccalaureate Degree, Re-Admit Students)

TRANSFER STUDENTS
William Paterson College accepts students for the fall and spring semesters (September and January) for full- or part-time study. When applying, students must present at least 12 college-level credits with a minimum 2.0 grade point average; accounting, business administration, computer science, economics and nursing majors must have at least a 2.5 GPA. Applicants who have completed fewer than 12 college credits must also submit a high school transcript. There are some limitations on the number of credits accepted, e.g., a maximum of 70 credits from a two-year college or 90 credits from a four-year college. More details on transferring credits may be obtained from our Admissions staff.

1. You must request that all colleges previously attended forward an official transcript of all college work completed to the Office of Admissions. The application form must show all courses in progress which will not appear on a transcript as submitted. To ensure accurate evaluations, applicants from out-of-state colleges should have appropriate catalogs sent to the Admissions Office.

2. Please include a copy of credit by examination, either CLEP or USAFI.

3. Credit will be transferred if:
   a. The college from which credits are to be transferred is on a list of approved colleges and universities.

b. They fit into the requirements or curriculum selected.

c. All post-high school work carries at least a 2.0 (C) cumulative grade point average on a four- (4) point scale.

4. Admission decisions are made on a rolling basis. Early application and early submission of all required records are advised as first-choice courses and housing space may be limited or gone before the application deadline.

5. Applicants admitted with 60 credits must declare a major and be accepted by a major department.

6. Applicants who have completed fewer than 12 transferable credits must submit SAT scores and an official high school transcript.

7. Student copies or unofficial copies of college transcripts will not be accepted for admissions purposes.

NOTE

1. In order to maintain quality programs and student services, the College will adhere to the printed deadlines. Failure to submit complete official records of all prior college coursework and high school transcripts, when required, will result in a delay in the application review process.

2. Transcripts received after your admission to the college and NOT listed on the application will not be accepted or reviewed for transfer credit.

RE-ADMIT STUDENTS

Students who have enrolled in undergraduate courses at WPC must file this application. If college courses have been completed at another college or university, an official copy of the transcript(s) must be forwarded to the WPC Office of Admissions. Certain College policies may require one to complete an additional form and/or supply further information resulting in a delay of the admissions process. Please submit application and all required documents as early as possible.

WPC students who exited the College in poor academic standing may be required to file an appeal with the dean of the school to which they are applying. Undeclared majors should appeal to the assistant vice president of academic affairs. Students uncertain of prior academic history should contact the registrar to obtain a copy of their transcript.

SECOND BACCALAUREATE DEGREE AT WILLIAM PATERSON COLLEGE

Students who already hold a baccalaureate degree may obtain a second baccalaureate degree in any nonteaching program. Applicants are considered upper-level division students and pay undergraduate fees. All credits earned through this program appear as undergraduate credits on the student's transcript. Students must complete all major requirements and collateral courses. A minimum of 30 credits must be completed at William Paterson College while enrolled in this program. Students who are nursing major must have completed the freshman requirements in order to be eligible for sophomore status in nursing.

SPECIAL ADMISSION

Educational Opportunity Fund Program (EOF)

The Educational Opportunity Fund program (EOF) is a special admissions and support program for students who are educationally underprepared and financially disadvantaged. The program is designed to provide comprehensive financial support and a broad range of educational and counseling assistance for all eligible students.

The program offers students the opportunity to begin their college experience in a summer program organized to help them become familiar with the academic demands of higher education, to strengthen basic skills and to gain exposure to the campus and college life. The EOF program also assists students in their personal and social adjustment to college. To be eligible, students must have been residents of New Jersey for the past year, demonstrate historical poverty and demonstrate potential for academic success. Additional information can be found on page VI.

EARLY ADMISSION

This program is available for highly motivated and academically exceptional students who have completed their junior year of high school and seek college admission. They may submit an application for early admission provided they meet the following criteria:

1. combined SAT scores of 1,000 or higher (or equivalent PSAT scores), and/or rank in the top 10 percent of their class, and/or exhibit exceptional talent in a special area;

2. receive the endorsement of a teacher or counselor;

3. submit a written essay describing their reasons for seeking early admission.

ADULT STUDENTS

Within the William Paterson College community there are a large number of adult or nontraditional students. Some are returning to school after a time lapse, some are taking courses to directly support their careers, and others come for personal enrichment. Most attend on a part-time basis with classes in the day, evening or on Saturday. Students who have not completed any college coursework and are 21 or older or have been out of high school for 2 years or more are considered nontraditional students. They must submit a high school transcript indicating graduation or copies of GED scores and diploma to be evaluated. An interview may be necessary before a decision is made. The Center for Continuing Education provides information on the services and programs available to adult students. For more information, please call (201) 595-2521.

INTERNATIONAL STUDENTS

Applicants from other countries are welcome at WPC. Admission is based on a review of the appropriate educational documents as well as proficiency in the English language as measured by the Test of English as a Foreign Language (TOEFL). To receive more detailed international student information, you may call or write:

International Admissions Officer
Office of Admissions
William Paterson College
Wayne, NJ 07470
Telephone (201) 595-2125

ADVANCED PLACEMENT

Some highly qualified entering freshmen may wish to take advanced level courses. This is acceptable if the student has an outstanding score in the appropriate subject in tests of either the CEEB or the College Board Achievement tests.

Eligibility for advanced placement may be established on the basis of scores on the Advanced Placement Examination of the College Board, College Level Examination Program (CLEP) or challenge examinations.

VETERANS

Credit awarded for certain courses taken while one is enlisted in the armed services may be applied toward a WPC baccalaureate degree. Veterans must submit a notarized copy of the DD214 or DD295, and official copies of high school and college transcripts along with the application. Contact the Office of Admissions for detailed information.

SCHOLARSHIPS AND FINANCIAL AID

Academic merit awards are offered to incoming freshmen. They are the Academic Excellence Scholarships, Trustee Scholarships and the African-American and Hispanic Student Scholarships. There are also numerous scholarships offered through academic departments. These scholarships are based not on need, but on academic performance. For a complete listing, refer to the WPC Scholarships and Financial Aid brochure. For a scholarship brochure, please call (201) 595-2125. Financial aid is available from state and federally funded programs. Distribution of funds (grants, loans and college work study) is based on need. Information and applications are available from the Financial Aid Office, (201) 595-2202.

STATEMENT OF POLICY

William Paterson College does not discriminate on the basis of race, color, age, sex, religion, creed, national origin, sexual orientation or disabling condition. College policies and practices are consistent with federal and state laws pertaining to equal opportunity in admissions and education policies and in scholarships, loans, athletics and other school-administered programs.

COUNTY CODES

Atlantic 01
Bergen 02
Burlington 03
Camden 04
Cape May 05
Cumberland 06
Essex 07
Gloucester 08
Hudson 09
Hunterdon 10
Mercer 11
Middlesex 12
Monmouth 13
Morris 14
Ocean 15
Passaic 16
Salem 17
Somerset 18
Sussex 19
Union 20
Warren 21
Delaware 23
Maryland 25
New York 30
Pennsylvania 40
Other 50

COMBINED FAMILY INCOME CODE

Code	Income Range
0	Less than $10,000
1	Between $10,001 and $19,999
2	Between $20,000 and $29,999
3	Between $30,000 and $39,999
4	Between $40,000 and $49,999
5	Between $50,000 and $59,999
6	Between $60,000 and $69,999
7	$70,000 and above

UNDERGRADUATE MAJORS AND CODES

Find your intended major on the list below. Write the name of the major, the assigned major code and the concentration code in the space provided on the undergraduate application. Please note that not every major has a minor code. Call the Admissions Hot Line for assistance with, and any questions you may have concerning, the application process: (201) 595-2125. For your convenience, two samples have been provided.

1. Major Biology
   Major Code: SH-B10-BS

2. Major: Undecided
   (no major selected)
   Major Code: SP-UND-UND
   Concentration Code: UND

NOTE: Elementary education (generalist, nursery-8th grade) certification is available to students selecting majors marked E. Secondary education (subject field specialization, K-12th grade) certification is available to students selecting majors marked S.

SCHOOL OF THE ARTS AND COMMUNICATION

	Major	Major Code	Concentration Code
E/S	Art/History	AC-ART-BA	HIST
E/S	Art/Studio	AC-ART-BA	STDO
	Fine Arts	AC-ART-BFA	
E/S	Communication*	AC-COMM-BA	
	Music Performance/Vocal	AC-MUSP-BM	VCE
	Music Performance/Instrument	AC-MUSP-BM	INST
S**	Music Certification/Vocal	AC-MUSC-BM	VCE
S**	Music Certification/Instrument	AC-MUSC-BM	INST
	Music Management	AC-MUS-BM	MGT
E	Music Studies	AC-MUS-BA	STDS
	Music Studies/Audio	AC-MUSJ-BM	AUD
	Music Jazz//Drum	AC-MUSJ-BM	JSD
	Music Jazz/Wind, Mallet, Guitar	AC-MUSJ-BM	JSW
	Music Jazz/Keyboard	AC-MUSJ-BM	JSK
	Music Jazz/Vocal	AC-MUSJ-BM	JSV
	Undeclared/Arts and Communication	AC-UND-UND	

* Communication: Interpersonal, Print Journalism
**Recognized as Music Education

SCHOOL OF EDUCATION

Major	Major Code	Concentration Code
Special Education	ED-SPED-BA	

Elementary and Secondary Education Certification Programs

Elementary and secondary education are professional preparation programs offered through the School of Education. Students interested in these programs must select a liberal arts major. Possible majors are indicated by the E (for elementary education, nursery-8th grade) or S (for secondary education, subject field specialization, K-12th grade). Formal acceptance into the professional preparation program leading to teacher certification will occur once the student has completed preliminary coursework at the College and has met acceptance criteria. (This usually occurs during sophomore year at the College.)

SCHOOL OF HUMANITIES, MANAGEMENT AND SOCIAL SCIENCES

	Major	Major Code	Concentration Code
	Accounting	HM-ACCT-BS	
E/S	African, African-American & Caribbean Studies	HM-AACS-BA	
	Anthropology	HM-ANTH-BA	
	Business Administration/Finance	HM-BUS-BS	FIN
	Business Administration/Management	HM-BUS-BS	MGT
	Business Administration/Marketing	HM-BUS-BS	MKT
E/S	English/Literature	HM-ENG-BA	LIT
E/S	English/Writing	HM-ENG-BA	WRIT
E/S	History	HM-HIST-BA	
E	Philosophy	HM-PHIL-BA	
E/S	Political Science	HM-POL-BA	
E	Psychology	HM-PSY-BA	
E/S	Sociology	HM-SOCI-BA	
E/S	Sociology/Applied	HM-SOCI-BA	APL
E/S	Sociology/Criminal Justice	HM-SOCI-BA	CJA
E/S	Sociology/Social Services	HM-SOCI-BA	SOS
E/S	Spanish	HM-SPAN-BA	
	Undeclared Humanities	HM-UND-UND	HUM
	Undeclared Management	HM-UND-UND	MGT
	Undeclared Social Science	HM-UND-UND	SS

SCHOOL OF SCIENCE AND HEALTH

	Major	Major Code	Concentration Code
E/S	Biology	SH-BIO-BS	
	Biotechnology	SH-BIOT-BS	
S	Community Health	SH-CSH-BS	
	Computer Science	SH-CS-BS	
E/S	Environmental Science	SH-ENV-BS	
E/S	Geography	SH-GEO-BA	
E/S	Mathematics	SH-MATH-BA	
S	Mathematics/Applied	SH-MATH-BA	APL
	Nursing	SH-NUR-BS	
S	Physical Education (K-12)*	SH-MSLS-BS	
	Physical Education Athletic Training	SH-MSLS-BS	
	Physical Education Exercise Physiology	SH-MSLS-BS	
	Undeclared Health	SH-UND-UND	HLT
	Undeclared Science	SH-UND-UND	SCI

*Formal acceptance into physical education concentrations will usually occur in the sophomore year once the student has completed preliminary coursework and has met acceptance criteria.

NO MAJOR SELECTED

Major	Major Code	Concentration Code
Undeclared	SP-UND-UND	UND

WILLIAM PATERSON UNIVERSITY
Application for Undergraduate Admission
Wayne, New Jersey 07470

Complete all items (print in ink or type).

ENCLOSE A $35 APPLICATION FEE–MONEY ORDER OR CHECK (FEE IS NONREFUNDABLE).

1. Social Security Number _____

2. Name in full _____

        LAST   FIRST   MIDDLE INITIAL

GIVE NAME IN FULL. DO NOT USE NICKNAMES OR ABBREVIATIONS.

IMPORTANT: Indicate any other last name under which transcripts may be received _____

3. Home Address _____

        NUMBER AND STREET

_____ 4. Phone No. _____

 CITY   STATE   ZIP   COUNTY

5. Date of birth _____ 6. Sex: _____ Male _____ Female   7. Are you a citizen of the U.S.? ____ Yes ____ No

        MONTH   DAY   YEAR

8. If you are not a U.S. citizen, what type of visa do you hold? _____

        (VISA HOLDERS PLEASE ATTACH COPY OF PASSPORT/ENTRY VISA/I-94)

9. If no, what is your country of citizenship? _____

10. Please indicate the answer that you feel best describes your race (required for federal reporting)

10. ____ White (W)   ____ Black/African-American (B)   ____ Asian/Pacific Islander (O)

    ____ American Indian/Alaskan Native (I)   ____ Hispanic (H)   Other (X) Specify: _____

11. County _____ Code _____ (see code sheet)

12. Are you a New Jersey resident? ____ Yes ____ No   13. Are you a veteran? ____ Yes ____ No

                                                    Are you active in the National Guard? ____ Yes ____ No

14. Are you a permanent resident of the U.S.A.? ____ Yes ____ No   Alien Registration No.: _____

                                                                                  (MUST INCLUDE COPY OF CARD)

15. Selecting your major—From the major code lists on page III, please indicate your major, major code and minor code (where required) in the spaces provided. (Students intending to pursue certification as teachers, must complete Item 15A below).

    Major _____ Major Code _____ Concentration Code _____

15A. Elementary Education (generalist, nursery-8th grade) and Secondary Education (subject field specialization, K-12th grade) are professional preparation programs offered through the School of Education. Students interested in becoming teachers should check their area of interest below. Special Education, which is a major, is also a professional preparation program.

I plan to pursue teacher certification through the School of Education in the area of:

     ____ Elementary Education (all subjects, nursery-8th grade)   ____ Special Education

     ____ Secondary Education (Subject field specialization, K-12th grade)   ____ Teaching (undecided about type of certification)

NOTE: Students interested in Elementary or Secondary Education must have a liberal arts major. Please select your liberal arts major noted by the E and/or S designation from the list on page III, and enter that major code on line 15.

16. What is your family's annual income? (Please see income codes on page III.) _____

17. Term: What semester do you plan to enroll?   September 19 ____   January 19 ____

18. Application type: (check one) ____ New Freshman ____ Transfer ____ Re-Admit ____ Second BA

     Status: (check one) ____ Part-Time ____ Full-Time

19. Please send me an EOF application; I may qualify for EOF (See income requirements on page VI): ____ Yes ____ No

20. Will you be applying for campus housing? ____ Yes ____ No

21. Academic history

High School _____

        NAME OF SCHOOL   CITY   STATE

High School CEEB# _____ Date of Graduation _____

Counselor's Name _____ Phone# _____

High school seniors must submit a FINAL high school transcript specifying date of graduation to the William Paterson College Office of Admissions. If you are not attending a school at the present time, please attach an explanation stating how you have been occupied since your last enrollment in school. Give brief details and dates.

IV

22. Are you presently attending or have you previously attended any college or university? ____Yes ____No
    If so, list institutions, locations and dates.

IMPORTANT:

1. Failure to provide a list of all colleges attended (including correspondence and extension courses) may result in delay in admission, loss of transfer credit and/or dismissal. It is the applicant's responsibility to have official transcripts forwarded from each college attended. An official report is required even though attendance was for a brief time and no credit was established.

2. Transcripts received after your admission to the college and **NOT** listed on the application will not be accepted or reviewed for transfer credit.

Please list in descending order beginning with current or most recent college.   DO NOT WRITE IN THESE BOXES

Name of Institution	Address (City and State)	CEEB#	Term Begin (Month & Year)	Term End (Month & Year)	Official Transcript Received	No. of Credits Attempted	GPA

Please use additional sheet if necessary.

23. **Please list your parents' name and address.**

Name   **Address**

_____

_____

24. I, the undersigned, state that the answers I have given to the questions in this application are complete and true.
    I agree to abide by the rules and regulations of William Paterson College.

Date _____ Signature of Applicant _____

RETURN TO: Office of Admissions, William Paterson College,
         300 Pompton Road, Wayne, New Jersey 07470

INFO. REQ.	DATE	DATE	DATE	FOR OFFICE USE—DO NOT WRITE IN THIS BOX			
				HS RANK	CLASS SIZE	PERCENTILE	
				SAT DATE	VERBAL	MATH	
				SAT DATE	VERBAL	MATH	
				GED DATE	SCORE	EOF READING	
APP FEE	DATE			ACADEMIC UNITS			
DEPOSIT FEE	DATE			TOEFL	DATE	SCORE	ADMISSIONS OFFICER DATE

EDUCATIONAL OPPORTUNITY FUND (EOF)

The Educational Opportunity Fund offers special admissions consideration to students who show academic promise, yet lack the educational and economic means to gain admission through traditional procedures. Educational support (tutorial) services as well as counseling are provided by the program. EOF also offers students the opportunity to begin their college experience in a summer enrichment program designed to familiarize them with the academic demands of higher education, strengthen their basic skills and assist them in adjusting to college life.

To apply for admission to William Paterson College through the Educational Opportunity Fund, you must meet specific academic and historical income requirements. Specific income requirements for 1996-97 are based upon the calendar year preceding application.

NOTE: Applicants may also qualify if they are:
■ a ward of the court
■ under legal guardianship
■ a welfare recipient
■ on disability.

If you wish to be considered for admission through the EOF program or to receive more information, please answer questions 16 and 19 on the admissions application. If you have any questions, please call (201) 595-2181.

The application and all supporting documents must be received by the appropriate deadlines.

DEPENDENT STUDENTS

A dependent student who comes from a family with both parents or guardians working and whose combined income exceeds the applicable amount set forth in the EOF Income Eligibility Scale may be eligible for EOF only if:

1. The total income does not exceed the applicable amount set forth in the EOF Income Eligibility Scale when 50 percent of the income of the smaller wage earner is subtracted from the gross combined income of the two wage earners; and

2. Documentation in each student's file includes the mathematical computation along with wage and tax statements (form W2) of both parents or guardians.

INDEPENDENT STUDENTS

An independent student is financially eligible for an EOF grant if the gross income of his or her parent(s) or guardian(s) does not exceed income limits set forth for dependent students.

1. An independent student's income is not to be added to that of his or her parent(s) or guardian(s), but the two incomes should be considered separately.

2. In cases where the independent student's parent(s) or guardian(s) is [are] receiving welfare support, parental income eligibility shall be presumed to have been met.

INCOME ELIGIBILITY CRITERIA
1995-96

Dependent Students Household Size	Estimated Gross Income
1 person	$14,940
2 persons	$20,060
3 persons	$25,180
4 persons	$30,300
5 persons	$35,420
6 persons	$45,660
7 persons	$50,780

Add $2,480 for each additional dependent.

NOTE Applicant must be a:
■ U.S. citizen or permanent resident, and
■ New Jersey resident for the last twelve (12) months

WPC

WILLIAM PATERSON UNIVERSITY
OFFICE OF ADMISSIONS (#1-62400)
300 POMPTON ROAD
WAYNE, NEW JERSEY 07470

Writing an Autobiography

Some job applications ask for a brief life history. (See Chapter 2 and Chapter 4 "Writing a Résumé" and "Writing a Biodata"). If you plan to apply to a college, you will almost surely have to write an autobiography, a history of your life. When you go for an interview, the interviewer almost always asks you to "tell about yourself."

Rationale

College applications often ask for an autobiography so the admissions committee can get a more complete picture of each potential student. Your autobiography does more than tell about your background and your plans for the future. It also shows your organizational and writing skills. Therefore, it's wise to write an outline first, even though the outline will never be sent to the college or seen by the interviewer. (See Chapter 9 for how to write an outline.) It's also important to consider who will be reading your autobiography. Knowing who your reading audience will be will help you focus your autobiography on those points you think will interest them most.

Materials Needed

practice paper, pen or pencil, typewriter or word processor, unlined paper or composition paper

Skills Involved

organizing material; writing an outline; writing paragraphs in sequential order; using correct spelling, capitalization, and punctuation

Important Vocabulary

autobiography a history of a person's life written by that person

extracurricular activities activities such as clubs and sports that students participate in outside of regular school hours

hobbies the things a person does for fun

skill the ability to do something well, usually developed by means of much practice

talent a natural ability; an ability one is born with

Example

AUTOBIOGRAPHY OF KIM CHUNG

I was born in Vietnam, that much I know, but about my birth I don't know much more. I was raised in an orphanage with other children whose parents were missing. The people in charge couldn't find my parents, but worse than that, they separated my twin sister and me and sent her to a different place. I will never stop looking for her.

When I was four years old, I was claimed by my American father and I spent the next six months at a refugee center in Thailand. Finally, when I was almost five years old, I came to the United States.

At first it was very difficult coming to this strange country. My father and his wife were very kind to me. Suddenly I had two brothers, Jerry and Johnnie. I was very nervous because I didn't look like anybody else in my family.

When I started school, there were many children from other countries and we all started to learn more about our new country, its culture, and its language. Everyone was very kind to me. My father's wife asked me to call her "Mom" the way my brothers did.

By the time I got to high school, I guess I was as American as I could be. I wore blue jeans and went to football games and had a part-time job at Burger King. My friends were Americans and Vietnamese and we all "hung out" together.

In my senior year of high school I met another Vietnamese whose story was similar to mine. He came to the United States when he was nine years old. He had many relatives here. He was working in his uncle's fruit and vegetable business when I met him. We were married six months after I graduated from high school.

Today, my husband, Lom, and I have two natural children. We have also adopted a Korean child and an American black child. We want to give as much love to as many children as we can in gratitude for our own good fortune.

I will search for my twin sister until I find her or have proof that she is no longer with us. My husband and I have worked very hard to make a good life for our children. He works many hours a day in our store. I take care of children of working parents in our home. Now I would like to go to college to learn how to run our business more efficiently so my husband wouldn't have to work so many hours. I want to study bookkeeping, accounting, and using a computer.

Procedure ▼

1. First make an outline for your autobiography. See Chapter 9 on how to write an outline.

2. If you are writing your autobiography as part of an application, be sure to follow any directions regarding content or format. Write or type a practice copy of your autobiography before you put it on the application form.

3. Begin with your beginnings, but unless there are very unusual circumstances, keep this section brief. Readers of applications have hundreds, sometimes thousands, of autobiographies to read. They are not interested in autobiographies that begin, "I was born at the stroke of midnight in the midst of a snowstorm," unless that snowstorm was of some special significance.

4. Go through your early years, noting anything particularly important or significant but keeping in mind that this part, too, should usually be brief.

5. If the autobiography is for a college application, the section that deals with your present activities and with your future plans will be most important to the college admissions board. Therefore, this section should be the longest and the most detailed. Include information about your hobbies, special skills and talents, and/or part-time jobs. If you are in high school, write about *why* you are taking certain courses, what extracurricular activities you're involved in, and any honors or awards you've received. Be sure to end with a paragraph about your plans for the future. If you are attending a community college or are working and not attending school at the time, tell something about your courses, the nature of your work, and your hobbies or other activities, as well as your plans for the future.

   If your autobiography is for a job application or some other purpose, focus on the parts of your life that will be most interesting to the reader and tell the most about the kind of person you are.

6. Proofread your practice copy to correct any spelling or punctuation errors. Rewrite any sentences you think you can improve. Then write or type your final copy.

7. Proofread your final copy and correct any errors. Because your autobiography is an introduction to you, be sure to take pride in its appearance.

Practice ▼

Now it's your turn.

Task: to write an autobiography. (See pages 82–92 for help in creating an outline before you begin writing your autobiography.)

Situation: You are filling out an application that calls for an autobiography. You may either type your autobiography or write it by hand.

8 Requesting an Interview

Whether you're applying for college or applying for a job, after you fill out the necessary application, you may be asked to come in for an interview. This is a meeting between you and a college admissions director or you and someone who is interested in hiring you for a job. Even if you aren't asked to come in for an interview, it's a good idea to request one yourself. An interview gives you the chance to demonstrate why you would be a good student or employee. Also, the person who interviews you will remember you better than if he or she had just read your cover letter and résumé or application.

Rationale

It is often easy and convenient to make an appointment for an interview by telephone. However, if you are applying for a job outside of your local area, or if you are requesting interviews at several different colleges, it makes more sense economically to write a short letter.

Another advantage to putting your request in writing is that you will have a better chance of reaching the person who is responsible for arranging an interview. That person may not be the one who answers the telephone if you call, and the message you leave may not be delivered correctly or—worse yet—may never get delivered at all. When you put your request in writing, the appropriate person will have all the important information in front of him or her and can either write or call you to set the time and date for your interview.

Materials Needed

unlined typing paper or stationery, pen, typewriter or word processor, envelope, postage stamp

Skills Involved

organizing thoughts; giving specific information; using correct spelling, punctuation, abbreviations, and capitalization

Important Vocabulary

application a form requesting information such as your name, address, telephone number, etc.

apply ask for; request

appointment a time and place arranged for people to meet

body the main part of a letter; the message

closing a word or phrase used to end a letter. The closing is found just above the writer's signature and is always followed by a comma.

hire assign a job to

indented form a format for writing letters in which the first line of each paragraph is placed farther in from the margin than the salutation

interview a meeting between two or more people. One person is usually at the interview for the purpose of applying for a job or admission to college. The other person or people are there to ask questions and to decide if the person being interviewed is right for the opening.

legible clear and easy to read

modified block form a format for writing letters in which the margins are the same from the first line to the end. Nothing is indented. A space is left between paragraphs.

responsible for in charge of

return address the address of the person sending a note or letter

salutation the greeting in a letter, usually beginning with *Dear* followed by a person's name

signature a person's name written in his or her own handwriting

Example

top margin	
return address	590 Park Ave. Middle Village, NY 11379 Nov. 23, 19—
right margin	Director of Admissions Boston University Boston, MA 02215
salutation	Dear Sir or Madam:
left margin	I expect to graduate from Middle Village High School in June of 19—. I would like to attend Boston University and would appreciate an interview with you. I will be in Boston the week of December 22–29 and wonder if you could see me sometime during that week. If not, I would appreciate an appointment at a time that is convenient for you. Because I'm still in school, I would appreciate a date at the beginning or end of a week, if possible. Thank you.
closing	Sincerely,
signature	*Beth Malovic*
typed name	Beth Malovic
bottom margin	

For an example of a cover letter requesting a job interview, see page 19.

Procedure A: Writing the Letter ▼

1. Use unlined stationery. If you have a typewriter or word processor available, it's always nice to type your letter. Typed letters look more professional and are easier to read. If you are writing your letter by hand, be sure your handwriting is legible and neat.

2.   Leave a margin on all four sides of the paper and center your letter so it looks attractive. If you are typing, use single spacing. Leave a space between

   - the return address and the address of the person you are writing to,
   - the address of the person you are writing to and the salutation,
   - the salutation and the body of the letter,
   - the body of the letter and the closing.

3.   Put your return address in the upper right corner, with your street name and number on the first line; the city, state, and zip code on the second line; and the date on the third line. If you use one abbreviation in the address, use appropriate abbreviations throughout. In other words, if you write Park *Ave.* instead of Park *Avenue*, then write Middle Village, *NY* instead of Middle Village, *New York*. Either style is correct. If you use abbreviations in the address, abbreviate the month when you write the date: *Nov.* 23, 19—. Your return address is necessary so the person who receives your letter will know where to send a response. You don't need to include your name here because it will appear at the bottom of your letter.

> 590 Park Ave.
> Middle Village, NY 11379
> Nov. 23, 19—

4.   Leave a space below the date. Then, on the left side of the paper, write the name or title of the person you are writing to and his or her address, following the same rules for abbreviations.

Director of Admissions
Boston University
Boston, MA 02215

5. Leave a space below the address. Then write *Dear* and the name of the person you are writing to on the left. If you don't know the person's name or whether you're addressing a male or female, write *Dear Sir or Madam.* Put a colon after the salutation.

> 590 Park Ave.
> Middle Village, NY 11379
> Nov. 23, 19—
>
> Director of Admissions
> Boston University
> Boston, MA 02215
>
> Dear Sir or Madam:

6. Ask for an appointment for an interview. If you are going to be in the area of the college or company at a particular time, or if you are only available for an interview at certain times, state that information clearly in your letter. Look at these examples.

    a. Indented Form

> I would appreciate an appointment for an interview during the Christmas vacation (December 22, 19— to January 3, 19—) or during our winter break, February 22–28, 19—, if possible.

    b. Modified Block Form

> I will be graduating from Middle Village High School in June 19— and would like to attend Boston University. I am available for an interview at your convenience. I would appreciate it if the interview could be on a Saturday or at the beginning or end of a week so I don't miss too much school. Thank you.

7.   Leave a space under your message. Then, on the right, end your letter with a word that shows your appreciation and interest. *Sincerely* is a good word because it is not too formal and it says that you mean what you wrote. Sign your full name under the closing. If you type your letter, be sure to leave enough space for your signature between the closing and your typed name.

Sincerely,

Beth Malovic

Beth Malovic

Your finished letter should look something like this:

590 Park Ave.
Middle Village, NY 11379
Nov. 23, 19—

Director of Admissions
Boston University
Boston, MA 02215

Dear Sir or Madam:

I expect to graduate from Middle Village High School in June of 19—. I would like to attend Boston University and would appreciate an interview with you. I will be in Boston the week of December 22–29 and wonder if you could see me sometime during that week. If not, I would appreciate an appointment at a time that is convenient for you. Because I'm still in school, I would appreciate a date at the beginning or end of a week, if possible. Thank you.

Sincerely,

Beth Malovic

Beth Malovic

Practice ▼

Now it's your turn.

Task: to write a letter requesting an appointment for an interview

Situation: You are a senior in high school. You would like to visit several colleges and have interviews with their directors of admissions. You are going to be in Providence, Rhode Island, during the week of February 12–19 and would like an interview at Brown University. The zip code for the school is 02906.

Remember the form:

_____

_____

_____

_____

_____

_____

_____ :

_____

_____

_____

_____

_____ ,

_____

Procedure B: Addressing the Envelope ▼

The name and address of the person you're writing to should be written or typed the same way inside the letter and on the envelope.

1.   Put your name and address (the *return address*) in the upper left corner of the envelope so that if the letter cannot be delivered for some reason, it will be returned to you.

2.   In the center of the envelope, write or type the name and address of the person you have written to. Put the person's name or title on the first line, the name of the college on the next line, and the city, state, and zip code on a third line. If you know the street name and number, put that information on a separate line just above the city, state, and zip code. If the letter is going outside the country you are writing from, be sure to put the name of the country on a fourth line.

3.   Put a postage stamp in the upper right corner. Be sure to use the correct amount of postage, or the letter will not be delivered.

   Your finished envelope should look something like this:

Ms. Beth Malovic
590 Park Ave.
Middle Village, NY 11379

Director of Admissions
Boston University
Boston, MA 02215

Practice B ▼

Now it's your turn.

Task: to address the envelope

Situation: You have written a letter requesting an interview. Now you want to mail it.

Procedure C: Folding the Letter ▼

See page 24 for instructions and diagrams describing the proper way to fold a letter before placing it in an envelope.

Practice C ▼

Now it's your turn.

Task: to fold your letter properly

Situation: You have proofread your letter, checking your spelling, punctuation, names, and addresses. Your envelope is addressed. Fold your letter and put it in the envelope.

Unit Three

Academic Writing

Making an Outline

Are you an organized person? Do you plan the night before what you are going to wear the next day? Do you make shopping lists? Do you schedule when you're going to do your homework or certain household tasks? Organized people get more done in less time. It's especially helpful to be organized when you have a paper to write. Knowing how to outline will help you see the benefits of (1) organizing your thoughts on paper and (2) being able to rearrange your ideas quickly and easily.

Rationale

An outline determines the shape or form of an essay, just as our skeletons determine the shape of our bodies. The amount and quality of the flesh on our skeletal frames affects the appearance of the final product, us. The amount of work we put into the "fleshing out" of an outline affects the quantity and quality of the final product, the essay. In both cases, it's important to begin with a good basic structure.

An outline is useful for any type of writing because it helps to organize one's thoughts in a logical or sequential order. In this chapter, we will focus on making an outline for an autobiography. However, the same procedure may be followed to make an outline for any type of writing.

Materials Needed

paper, pen or pencil

demonstrating knowledge of alphabet and number sequence, using parallel construction, organizing thoughts

Important Vocabulary

autobiography a history of a person's life written by that person

capital letters letters taking the form *A*, *B*, *C*, and so forth

essay a relatively short piece of writing, usually on one subject

extracurricular activities activities such as clubs and sports that students participate in outside of regular school hours

flesh the skin that covers our bones

flesh out to develop or add to

hobbies the things a person does for fun

logical order an order that makes sense. (If you are writing your autobiography, a *logical order* would be to start with your birth and continue through your lifetime to the present. At the end you might discuss the future.)

lowercase letters letters taking the form *a*, *b*, *c*, and so forth

parallel construction using the same grammatical form to express all items in a list of two or more items being compared. (*She likes skating, reading, and cooking* shows parallel construction, while *She likes skating, reading, and to cook* does not.)

rearrange put in a different order

uppercase letters capital letters

Examples

See the following pages.

a. Outline for Autobiography of Juan Mendoza

I. Birth
   a. Where
   b. When
II. Early years
   a. School
   b. Friends
   c. Moves
      1. Venezuela
      2. Brooklyn
III. Teen years
   a. School
      1. Subjects
      2. Extracurricular activities
         a. Spanish club
         b. Student council
   b. Hobbies
      1. Guitar
      2. Band
      3. Soccer
   c. Part-time job
IV. Plans for future
   a. College
   b. Career
   c. Family

A typical outline for the autobiography of a high school student might look something like Example a on page 84. Juan Mendoza was born in one country but moved to two other countries when he was six years old, so he has included a section about "moves" in his early years. As a high school student writing his autobiography for a college application, he has included sections about the most important aspects of his high school career and also his plans for the future.

When Juan writes his autobiography, he will look at his outline and know (1) where to begin, and (2) what to include and in what order. He won't have to trust his ideas to memory because his outline tells him what to include in his essay. The opening paragraph for his essay might look something like this:

I was born in Cali, Colombia, on June 7, 1972. I spent my earliest years in Cali and started school there. I still remember my special friends even though my family moved to Venezuela when I was only six. We lived in Venezuela for a few months and then we moved again, this time to Brooklyn, New York. It was very different from Cali...

b. Outline for Autobiography of Kim Chung

I. Birth
II. Early years
  A. Orphanage
    1. Search for parents
    2. Separation from twin sister
  B. Thailand
  C. U.S.A.
III. Teen years
  A. New family
  B. High school
  C. Friends
  D. Job
IV. Present
  A. Family
    1. Husband
    2. Natural children
    3. Adopted children
      a. Korean
      b. Black
  B. Search for twin sister
  C. Career
  D. College
V. Plans for future

Kim Chung is a young mother with two natural children and two adopted children. She takes care of children of working parents in her home, but she really wants to go to college. She'd like to study bookkeeping, accounting, and using a computer. Her autobiography for a college application might start like this:

> I was born in Vietnam, that much I know, but about my birth I don't know much more. I was raised in an orphanage with other children whose parents were missing. The people in charge couldn't find my parents, but worse than that, they separated my twin sister and me and sent her to a different place. I will never stop looking for her.
>
> When I was four years old, I was claimed by my American father and I spent the next six months at a refugee center in Thailand. Finally, when I was almost five years old, I came to the United States.

The fact that Kim has a family of her own now and that she is very sensitive about her own early years will make the fleshing out of number IV in her outline extremely important. This part of her autobiography will help a college admissions committee to see why she has waited until now to pursue college and to plan for the career she has chosen.

Procedure ▼

Below are some simple points to remember when writing an outline:

1. The basic structure of an outline is, in sequential order:
    a. Roman numerals
    b. capital letters indented under Roman numerals
    c. Arabic numerals indented a little more
    d. lowercase letters indented a little more

There should never be a *I* without a *II*, never an *A* without a *B*, never a *1* without a *2*, and never an *a* without a *b*.

You can use as many letters and numbers as you wish.

2. Specific information is not usually given in an outline. Save the details for the writing of the essay.

3. Use as few words as possible for each point. Remember to use parallel construction. Sample format for an outline:

I.

   A.

   B.

      1.

      2.

      3.

         a.

         b.

II.

III.

   A.

      1.

      2.

   B.

      1.

      2.

   C.

      1.

      2.

         a.

         b.

         c.

4.   Whether the topic for your outline is one you have chosen or one you have been assigned, the procedure is the same.

    a.   Make a list of the main points you want to include. (These are the points that will probably become topic sentences in your essay.) Put them in the order you want to talk about them and number them with Roman numerals (I, II, III, IV, etc.).

        For example, if your outline is about winter weather in the United States, you might divide your information something like this:

Winter Weather in the United States
I.   North
II. East
III. South
IV. West

    b.   Go back to each major topic and list under it the most important points you want to make about that topic. Put these points in a logical order and give each one a capital letter.

        For example, you could describe the weather in various sections of each large area:

I.   North
   A.   Northeastern states
   B.   North Central states
   C.   Northwestern states

c.   Under each letter, use Arabic numerals to include more specific details:

I.   North
    A.   Northeastern states
        1.   Rainfall
        2.   Snowfall
        3.   Temperature highs
        4.   Temperature lows

d.   You can include still more information using lowercase letters:

I.   North
    A.   Northeastern states
        1.   Rainfall
        2.   Snowfall
           a.   amount each year
           b.   effect on people's lives, jobs, etc.

5.   After you finish your outline, look at it carefully.

- Is your information in good sequential order?

- Did you use parallel construction? (For example, did you use the same part of speech for all the letters under Roman numeral I?)

6.   Rearrange your outline until it is just the way you want it. Keep it right in front of you and use it as a guide when you write your essay. Follow its order and remember:

- Every Roman numeral in your outline should be the beginning of a new paragraph in your essay.

- Don't use the numbers or letters in your essay; they are just guides for you.

7.   Your outline is just for you. Its purpose is to help you include all that you want to say in your paper in a logical, interesting manner.

Now it's your turn.

Task: to write an outline for an autobiography

Situation: You are applying for college or for a job. You have been asked to write an essay telling about yourself, your background, interests, education, plans for the future, and anything else that might help the people who read your autobiography decide if you are the kind of person they are looking for. Write an outline for your autobiography.

10 Writing an Essay

The word *essay* has many meanings. Two of the most important definitions of *essay* as the word is used in school are as follows:

- a one-paragraph (or longer) written answer to a test question

- several paragraphs written about a subject, in which the writer expresses his or her opinions or tries to make certain points, using details and facts to support each idea or opinion.

A book report is one kind of essay. (See pages 100–107 for an example.) A written review of a movie or TV program is also an essay.

Rationale

Knowing how to write an essay can open a variety of careers to you as a writer/columnist or reviewer for newspapers, magazines, radio, and/or television, to name just one type of professional opportunity. Educationally, the ability to write good essay answers to test questions is becoming more and more important as educators and members of the business community recognize the need for people to be able to express themselves in an intelligent, organized fashion. Other chapters in this book also deal with various forms of essay writing. (See Chapter 7 and Chapter 11 "Writing an Autobiography" and "Writing a Book Report.") This section focuses on essay answers to test questions.

Materials Needed

practice paper, pencil or pen and composition paper, or typewriter/word processor and unlined paper

Skills Involved

organizing ideas and information; supplying specific details or facts to support ideas and information; writing sentences and paragraphs (writing a topic sentence with supporting details in following sentences); using correct spelling, punctuation, and capitalization

Important Vocabulary

columnist a person who writes essays on topics of his or her choice for a newspaper or magazine

concluding ending; the concluding sentence is the last sentence

mass media methods of communication such as radio, television, newspapers, and magazines that are designed to reach many, many people at once

personnel the people who work for an organization

reviewer a person who gives his or her opinion (orally or in writing) on a recent book, play, musical, radio or television show, or other event for one of the mass media

supporting details specific facts or information that can be used to prove what you're saying is true

topic sentence a sentence that states the main idea of a paragraph, often the first sentence

Example

Test question:

How can schools get parents to work more closely with them in the education of their children?

Essay answer:

One thing school personnel have to realize is that there may be many reasons why parents don't come to school. The fact that they don't come to school doesn't necessarily mean they don't care about their children or they aren't helping their children at home. Some parents may not come to school to talk to teachers because they work during school hours. Parents who have come here from other countries may not come to school because they don't speak English or they are embarrassed by their accents and their limited English. Other parents may not come to school because they don't have anyone to take care of their babies. Many parents from other countries think the schools know what is best for their children and believe they are not supposed to come to school to ask questions. Questioning their children's teachers is not something they would do in their native countries. They think of school personnel as professionals who know their jobs and who shouldn't be bothered by parents, or who might even be angry or insulted if parents dared to question them.

topic sentence

supporting details

There are ways for schools to help parents to work more closely with them in the education of their children. Schools can send home bilingual messages in English and in the parents' native language announcing meetings, suggesting ways of helping their children, giving parents information they should have, and asking parents if they have any questions. Schools can also arrange meetings between parents and teachers at times that are convenient for both groups, providing some kind of volunteer baby-sitting service in the school so parents with younger children can attend. Another thing schools can do is to have teachers visit groups of parents in one parent's home, to discuss problems and solutions on the parents' home ground. That would probably make the parents feel more comfortable. It would take a lot of planning, but it would be good because it would also give teachers and other school personnel who attend a chance to see where and how their students live. School personnel would become better educated about their students and this would help them in their future planning.

topic sentence

supporting details

concluding sentence

Procedure ▼

When writing an essay answer to a test question, you should:

1. Study ahead of time for the test.

2. Read the test question carefully and, on a separate piece of paper, write down in abbreviated form all the relevant information that comes to your mind. Even if this is a timed test, you'll still have time to organize and complete your essay because your notes are not in complete sentences; they are more like an outline of what you want to remember to include in your answer.

   For example, if the question is on a history test and you are asked how various wars affected United States foreign policy, you first want to remember as many wars as possible that you studied in class. You might write down their names as they come into your head:

Fr-Ind
1812
Rev
Civil
WW1
WW2
Korean
Vietnam
Span-Amer

   (The abbreviations refer to the French and Indian War, the Revolutionary War, World Wars I and II, and the Spanish-American War.)

   When you refer to this list, put the wars in the correct *chronological* order (the order in which they occurred), and write about how each one affected United States foreign policy. This method is easier than having to stop and think after you write about each war, and it reduces your chances of leaving one out.

3. After you write your topic sentence for each paragraph, be sure to give as many reasons or facts as you can to support what you've written. See the topic sentences and supporting details in the example on page 95.

4.　At the end of your essay, write a concluding sentence to summarize what you've said: for example, *This shows how the United States' foreign policy has been affected by various wars the country has been involved in.*

5.　Proofread, if you have time. Correct and rewrite whatever you feel needs improving. Be sure you have proved your points.

Practice ▼

Now it's your turn.

Task:　to answer an essay question

Situation:　You are taking a test and must answer this question:

How can an understanding of various cultures help us in our personal and professional lives? Use your own experience and the experiences of people you know or have read about to prove your points.

Writing a Book Report

Have you ever heard or read something about a book that made you really want to read that book? Or have you ever read a book you couldn't wait to tell someone else about, either because you enjoyed it so much or because you were so disappointed in it?

Newspapers and magazines often publish book reviews that make people feel they must get a certain book immediately or decide this is one book they're really not interested in reading. Television news programs often talk about new books, movies, or plays people should know about. The reviewers tell why they liked or didn't like each play, movie, or book and then give some examples to prove their points. In the media, these are called *reviews*. In school, they're usually called *reports*. This chapter is about writing one kind of report—a book report.

Rationale

There are many reasons for writing a book report. A major reason is to share something about a book with other people so they can decide if they would like to read the book. Writing book reports improves our organizational and writing skills, helps us recognize the most important points an author is making, and gives us an opportunity to express our opinions. It may even lead to a career as a reviewer for a newspaper, a magazine, or a radio or television station.

Materials Needed

pen, practice paper, composition paper or typewriter/word processor and unlined paper

Skills Involved

reading comprehension; organizing thoughts; evaluating what you've read; expressing opinion; offering supporting details; summarizing; using correct spelling, capitalization, and punctuation

Important Vocabulary

accomplishments things a person has done

autobiography a history of a person's life written by that person

biography a history of a person's life written by someone else

conclusion a final decision, based on certain facts and feelings

evaluating deciding for yourself the value or quality of something

expressing opinion telling how you feel about something

expressions words and phrases used for saying something

fiction a story that the author has imagined

gestures facial or body movements used for communication

nonfiction a piece of writing that is true

parentheses punctuation marks ( ) used to show that certain information is interesting or useful but not absolutely necessary

plot the plan for a story; the events that take place in a story

summarizing telling in a few words or sentences the main ideas of a larger piece of writing

supporting details specific facts or information that can be used to prove what you're saying is true

theme the topic or subject of a story

Example

Review of
Everyday Japanese by Edward Schwarz and Reiko Ezawa

topic sentence — Everyday Japanese, A Basic Introduction to the Japanese Language and Culture is divided into three parts, each of which gives the reader a clearer picture of life in modern Japan. Part One, "Getting Around in Japan," gives general conversation and introductions and teaches the non-Japanese-speaking person how to buy a ticket at the train station, take a taxi, check in and out of a hotel, make appointments, shop, and be **specific details** understood at the doctor's office, the drugstore, the post office, and so forth. All the "Useful Expressions" are written both in the Roman alphabet and in Japanese, with the English translation in parentheses. The pronunciation of the letters in Japanese and the symbols used are explained in the introduction. It is very important that the reader begin Everyday Japanese by reading all the material before Part One.

Part Two, "Only in Japan," teaches the reader important expressions and correct behavior at a tea ceremony, theater and sporting events, temples and shrines, and in a Japanese house. It also teaches about Japanese holidays and festivals, clothing, and the Japanese bath. Students not only learn the appropriate words, phrases, and behavior for various places and occasions; they also learn the history or reasons behind each activity and behavior. They learn the language and the culture, as the book says in its title.

Part Three of the book is about "Living in Japan" and is very important for people planning to move there from another country. It has useful expressions in sections on the immigration office, buying or renting a house or an apartment, automobiles, gestures, and counting in Japanese.

Every section of Everyday Japanese has an illustration and a vocabulary list of twenty words. There are useful expressions and dialogues to practice, and notes that tell about the culture and why things are done a certain way.

I liked this book because I'm interested in learning the Japanese language and also because I like to learn about other cultures. I found it very interesting that <u>karate</u> means "empty hand" and that a karate expert can break bricks and piles of wood with his bare hand. I also found it interesting that the Japanese take off their shoes before entering a house. The Japanese can fold up their beds, called <u>futons</u>, and put them away when they get up in the morning. The most fascinating thing to me was that before the Japanese take a bath, they wash themselves <u>outside</u> the tub. The tub is kept clean and can be used more than once before the water is changed.

specific details

I would recommend this book to anyone who wants to learn something about Japanese culture. People who would like to learn some useful Japanese expressions for traveling or living in Japan would also find <u>Everyday Japanese</u> helpful.

conclusion

Myra Androyan

Procedure ▼

If your teacher has given you a list of questions to answer about the book, or has given you specific directions for how the report is to be written, be sure to follow those directions carefully. Usually you will be asked to write a summary of the book and to tell why you did or didn't like it. It is always best to write a practice copy first so you can correct your mistakes and rewrite any sentences you don't like. You can also take out anything you decide is not necessary and check to make sure that you have given examples to support your opinions. Here are some general guidelines for writing a book report:

1. Give the title and author of the book. It's often a good idea to include the name of the publisher (the company that printed the book) and the year it was published.

2. Begin by telling something about the book.

   • Is it fiction or nonfiction?

   • Is it divided in a way that is important for the reader to know?

3.   If the book is fiction:

- Tell something about the characters and how they are involved in the story.

Don't tell too much about the plot or the ending, but try to make the reader want to read the book by describing something you found really exciting or fascinating. This is called "creating suspense," making the reader wonder what happens next. If no such excitement occurred for you, you can say this too, again using examples to show why the author didn't accomplish his or her purpose.

- Tell whether the characters and the plot were believable. Use examples to explain why or why not.

- Tell something about what you liked and/or didn't like about this book. What made you choose it?

4.   If the book is nonfiction:

- Tell what kind of book it is (autobiography, biography, history book, travel book, etc.).

If it's an autobiography or a biography, explain what made this person worthy of having a book written about him or her. Name some of the person's specific accomplishments. Tell how you felt about this person when you finished reading the book. Why did you feel this way? Be very specific, giving details from the book to illustrate (explain) your points.

If the book you read was a history book, tell something about the period of time covered and why a book was written about it. Describe your reactions to this period and the events that took place. Would you like to have lived at that time? Why or why not? Be specific.

If the book you read was a travel book, tell something about the places described in the book. Explain why the author wrote about those particular places. Now that you've read the book, tell why you would or wouldn't want to visit or live in those places. Be specific, giving examples or details from the book to support your opinions.

- Explain what you liked and/or didn't like about the book. What made you choose it?

5.   Avoid overusing the word *interesting* when you tell how you feel about a book. This word is used so much it has lost its meaning. If you found the book exciting, give an

example of *what* was exciting. If it was boring, show *why*, with an example. A good book report is a combination of "tell" and "show." You want the readers of your book report to believe what you're saying, so after you *tell* what you think and how you feel, *show* why you feel this way by giving some specific details or facts.

6.   End your report by telling why you would or would not recommend this book to others. Be specific about your reasons.

Practice ▼

Now it's your turn.

Task: to write a book report

Situation: You have been assigned to write a book report. Choose a book you have read recently and write a report about it.

12 Academic Writing

Taking Notes from a Lecture

Whether you're in school or not, you probably find yourself attending a lecture, speech, meeting, debate, or class at least occasionally. Often, you want to remember the speaker's most important points so you can study for a future exam, use the information in an essay or research paper, ask questions or challenge a point, or have a record of what was said for use in a future meeting or debate. One way to remember the most important points of any talk is to take notes on what the speaker says.

Rationale

It isn't easy to take notes when someone is speaking, because you usually can't go back and have things repeated and because you have to keep listening to the next thing being said while you're writing down what you've just heard. For these reasons, some people take tape recorders to classes or lectures so they can record what is being said, but this is not always a good idea. You must have the speaker's permission to tape, and he will not always give it, for a variety of reasons. Even if you have permission, sometimes the sound is not good and you can't understand what is on the tape afterward, or there are other noises on the tape that make it hard to hear. You may get a lot of information you do not want or need, and you have to spend time listening to the whole talk again as you pick out the material you want. Finally, relying on a tape recorder can make you lazy and leave you with a big problem if the machine breaks or isn't available. It's important to develop your listening and concentration skills, along with your note-taking skills.

Materials Needed

notebook, pens or pencils

Skills Involved

listening comprehension; concentration; recognizing and summarizing key thoughts; being able to listen and write at the same time

Important Vocabulary

abbreviation a shortened form of a word; for example, *Dr.* for *doctor, appt.* for *appointment*

concentration keeping your mind on the subject you are listening to or reading about

debate a discussion between two or more people who don't agree on a subject. Each person tries to prove that his or her opinion is correct.

lazy not wanting to work

lecture a talk given by a professor or other authority on a subject

relying depending

taking notes writing down in abbreviated form what you want to remember from something you're reading or hearing

tape recorder a small machine that can record sound on a special kind of tape and can play that sound back later

Example

Your teacher will read or play the sample lecture for you. Remember, you will hear the lecture only once, and at a normal speaking rate, so listen carefully. If you are studying independently, the text of the lecture is printed in Appendix A. You can look at the text and take notes from it, although this is not the same as hearing it. In either case, write down what you think are the most important points on a piece of scrap paper.

Your notes from the lecture might look like this:

> ### Amer. Table Manners—3/1—Stacia St. Claire
>
> Amer. din. cust. diff. from other places. (1) Guests arr. on time. (2) Fork mostly in rt. hand. (3) Don't use knife to help. (4) Knife for cut. meat, pot. (5) Knife to rt. of plate when not using. (6) Napkin on lap. (7) Some food eaten w/ fingers, espec. at picnics, etc.

Naturally, you would use your own form of shorthand and abbreviations, but see if you can make sense out of these notes since you have heard or read the actual lecture. The first information given is the subject of the talk (American table manners), the date of the lecture (March 1), and the name of the speaker. Notice the period (.) at the end of each abbreviation.

Procedure ▼

1. Have your notebook and pen or pencil ready.

2. Before the speaker begins, write the date and title or subject of the lecture or class. If the person giving the lecture is not your regular teacher, you might want to write the speaker's name, too.

3. Listen for the main idea and examples to prove it. Write these down as you hear them.

4. Abbreviate words and use your own shorthand. You don't have to number your notes, but you may do so if it will help to organize them. They are numbered in the example above because each numbered statement represents an example of the main idea that "American dining customs differ from those in other places."

5. Write only the most important facts.

   It is very good practice to listen to newscasts on the radio and take notes from them. Since the same news is often broadcast several times a day, you can check your notes at different times to see how complete and accurate they are.

Practice ▼

Now it's your turn.

Task: to take notes from a lecture

Situation: You are attending a lecture on test-taking. Listen to the lecture* and take notes on the most important points. Remember, you will hear the lecture only once and at a normal speaking rate, so concentrate on what is being said as you write.

*Your teacher will read or play the lecture for you. If you are studying independently, see Appendix A for the text of the lecture. Try to find someone to read it to you so you can practice taking notes in a listening situation. If there is no one to read the conversation to you, look at the text and take notes from it, remembering that this is not quite the same as hearing the words without being able to see them or have them repeated.

13

Taking Notes from a Reading

When you read a book, article, or other piece of writing, you often want to remember the main points of what you've read. One way to do this is by taking notes as you read. Later, when you want to remember what the book or article was about, you can look at your notes instead of reading the whole thing again.

Rationale

If you're in school, it's a good idea to take notes whenever you read an assignment from a textbook or other source. Then you can use your notes to study before a test or final exam. Even if you're not in school, you probably read books or articles related to your work, hobbies, or other interests. Taking notes as you read gives you a record of what you have read that you can review at any time.

Materials Needed

textbook or other reading material, pen or pencil, notebook or index cards (3" × 5" or larger)

Skills Involved

reading comprehension; using abbreviations; recognizing topic sentences, key words, and key phrases; summarizing; recognizing what's important for a particular situation (for example, what material you need to study for a particular exam or what facts you need to prove a certain point)

Important Vocabulary

abbreviation a shortened form of a word; for example, *Dr.* for *doctor, appt.* for *appointment*

key words most important words

points ideas you want people to know, think about, and/or understand

shorthand a form of writing that uses special signs, letters, and abbreviations to make note-taking easier and faster (*&* for *and* and *w* for *with* are forms of shorthand.)

single only one

source a person, place, or object that contains information

summarize tell in a few words or sentences the main ideas of a larger piece of writing

taking notes writing down in abbreviated form what you want to remember from something you're reading or hearing

topic sentence a sentence that states the main idea of a paragraph, often the first (or sometimes the last) sentence

Example

Read this information on "Alphabetical Order," then look at the notes taken from it.

ALPHABETICAL ORDER[1]

There are twenty-six letters in the English alphabet. Every English student should know the alphabet. The letters are abcdefghijklmnopqrstuv wxyz. It is important to know the order of the alphabet. It is often used to organize books and parts of books. It helps you find words in a dictionary, for example. It helps you find which book to use in an encyclopedia of many books.

Sometimes alphabetical order uses only the letters, like this: A–E; F–I; J–L; M–O; P–S; T–Z. Sometimes, especially in a library, alphabetical order is by the first letter of names or words....

[1]Margaret Martin Maggs, *English Across the Curriculum 2* (Lincolnwood, IL: National Textbook Co., 1983) 1–3.

In alphabetical order, sometimes there are two words that begin with the same letter. An example of this is **and** and **apple.** What do you do then? You use the second letter to help you alphabetize (put in alphabetical order). In the word **and** the second letter is **n.** In the word **apple** the second letter is **p. n** is before **p** in the alphabet. The word **and** is before **apple** in alphabetical order.

Notes from a single source can be put either in a notebook or on index cards. Whichever you use, be sure to include the necessary information about the source. The notes shown below are in a notebook. For longer reports, index cards are easier to use, as you will see in the next chapter.

<u>English Across the Curriculum 2</u>
Margaret Martin Maggs
National Textbook Co., Lincolnwood, IL 1983 pages 1–3

26 letters in Eng. alphabet. All Eng. students should know alpha. Imp. know order of alpha. Used to organize books, dict., encycl. Sometimes only lttrs used on bks. When 1st let. of wds same, wds alpha. by 2nd let., e.g., <u>an</u>d, <u>ap</u>ple.

Cover the reading and look only at the notes. Can you make any sense out of them? It will be easier to read your own notes, of course, because you will have your own way of abbreviating. Without looking at the original reading, see if you can write a few sentences just from the notes. When you're finished, look at the reading again. Did you get the main idea? What kind of notes would you have taken?

Procedure ▼

1. Look at the end of the chapter or section you are preparing to read. Are there questions to be answered? These questions are often the key to the main points of the reading. *Read the questions first.* Then, when you read the chapter, the most important points will "jump out" at you. You'll be able to answer the questions and

you'll know what the author considers most important. These are the points that you'll especially want to take notes on.

2.   Use your own shorthand and abbreviations to take notes. For example, don't write words like *a*, *and*, or *the*. Abbreviate words like *information (info.)*, *association (assoc.)*, *with (w)*, and *including (incl.)*. One easy way to abbreviate is to leave out the vowels (*a, e, i, o, u*) in some words; for example, *signed* becomes *sgnd*. The important thing is to use abbreviations that you are comfortable with and that you will remember the meaning of when you need to read your notes again at a later date.

3.   Don't use complete sentences in your notes. If a sentence in the article reads

The Declaration of Independence of the United States of America was signed by many important people, including Thomas Jefferson, John Hancock, and Benjamin Franklin.

your notes might read,

Dec. of Ind. sgnd by mny imp. ppl, incl. T. Jefferson, J. Hancock, B. Franklin.

If you don't think you'll remember the men's first names, you might shorten Jefferson's to *Tom* and Franklin's to *Ben*.

4.   Keep your notes in a notebook and write them in ink so they'll be easy to read when you want to study from them at a future date.

5.   It's always a good idea to mark down the name of the book and the pages you took your notes from. You may also want to list the chapter number and/or title so you can turn back to it quickly when you need to.

6.   When you finish taking notes, always read them over to be sure they make sense to you. If you don't understand something now, it's going to be a lot harder to

understand a week or a month from now. Go back to the reading and see what you meant to write. Then fix your notes while it's easy to do so.

Practice ▼

Now it's your turn.

Task: to take notes from a reading

Situation: You have been assigned to read the passage from *The Birthday of the United States* by Gustavo Maja (Austin, Texas: Voluntad Publishers, 1979) on the following page. Take notes to answer the questions on page 119.

Countries have birthdays, just as you and I do.

And every year the United States has a giant birthday party.

The United States' birthday is the 4th of July.

This is the story of the birth of the United States.

Many years ago, the American states were not united. They were part of a country called Great Britain. All the laws were made far away by King George the Third. King George made everyone pay him a lot of money in taxes. The people in the American colonies did not like the laws. Samuel Adams and Thomas Paine loved America. They wanted America to be free to make its own laws. They spoke to many Americans about their ideas. They wanted America to be a new country.

King George sent soldiers to make the ideas stop. Instead there was a war. Paul Revere rode his horse all one night to warn people that the soldiers were on their way. They quickly got up and armed themselves to fight for their freedom.

The soldiers sent by King George wore beautiful uniforms. These British soldiers came from faraway Great Britain to fight against the American colonies and make them obey King George's laws.

The American patriots were not soldiers. They did not wear uniforms, but they were very brave people. They fought against the soldiers so the colonies could be free states. They fought for the right to unite and form a new nation.

The war for independence was long and very hard. Some of the patriots gathered together; their meeting was called a congress. Thomas Jefferson wrote a letter—a Declaration of Independence—and they all signed it. Some of the signers were Benjamin Franklin, Samuel Adams, and John Hancock.

The Declaration listed all the problems that King George had caused the people in the colonies. It also said that everyone should have a chance to give an opinion. That idea is called democracy. The Declaration of Independence was signed on the 4th of July more than two hundred years ago.

The war was not over yet, but that letter was the birth of the United States of America. It was born during a war, but the war was won later. And every year that birthday is celebrated by Americans living all over the world. It is a day of great joy. Flags can be seen everywhere.

The flag now has fifty stars—one for each free state. And it has thirteen stripes—one for each of the colonies that fought the war for independence.

The 4th of July is the biggest national holiday. There are parades, picnics, music, and parties everywhere. Stores close, and people go camping and visit their friends. In the evening there are fireworks for everyone to enjoy. It is the biggest birthday party of the year. It is a celebration of the signing of the Declaration of Independence on the 4th of July many years ago. It is the birthday of the United States of America.

Questions:
1. When is the United States' birthday?
2. What is the Declaration of Independence?
3. Who are some of the men who signed the Declaration?
4. Who was Paul Revere?
5. What are "patriots"?
6. Who was king of Great Britain during the time of the war?

Read over your notes. Write a paragraph or two from your notes. Check what you've written against the original reading. How accurate and complete are your notes?

Did you remember to look for questions at the end before you began your reading? Answer the questions now. Are they easy to answer from your notes? If not, go back through the reading and see what important points you missed.

14

Taking Notes from Multiple Sources

When you read more than one book or talk to more than one person about a particular topic, it's easy to forget later where you read or heard a certain piece of information. If you plan to write a paper or give a speech on that topic, it's important to know where you got every piece of information you use. Taking notes as you read or listen will give you a record of all your information and where it came from.

Rationale

During the course of your education, you will probably have to write more than one term paper or research paper. These kinds of papers usually require you to use information from many different sources. When you are collecting facts for a report or presentation of any kind, it's hard to rely on memory alone. Therefore, it's important to learn good note-taking skills.

Materials Needed

pen or pencil, reading materials, index cards (3" × 5" or larger)

Skills Involved

reading comprehension; using abbreviations; recognizing topic sentences, key words, and key phrases; summarizing; recognizing what you need to know for a particular situation (for example, what material you need to study for a particular exam or what facts you need to prove a certain point)

abbreviation a shortened form of a word; for example, *Dr.* for *doctor*, *appt.* for *appointment*

author writer

bibliography a list of sources appearing at the end of a book, article, research paper, or other reading. The title, author, publisher, publication date, and pages for each source are noted.

footnoting making a note at the bottom of a page to tell where you got a certain piece of information

index cards small white cards, usually lined on one side and unlined on the other. The most common size is 3" × 5" (three inches by five inches).

key words most important words

multiple many; more than one

points ideas you want people to know, understand, and/or think about

quote one person's words repeated exactly in a piece of writing or speech by another person. Whenever you use a quote in a paper, you must use quotation marks (**" "**) around the exact words that you are quoting. You must also give credit to the person you are quoting, usually in a footnote.

research looking for and reading information from many sources about a particular topic

research paper a paper that is several pages long, usually dealing with one subject in depth and based on information learned through research

shorthand a form of writing that uses special letters, signs, and abbreviations to make note-taking easier and faster (*&* for *and* and *w* for *with* are forms of shorthand)

source a person, place, or object that contains information

summarize tell in a few words or sentences the main ideas of a larger piece of writing

taking notes writing down in abbreviated form what you want to remember from something you're reading or hearing

term paper a paper on a particular subject, usually due near the end of a school term. It requires research, footnotes, and a bibliography.

title the name of a book, speech, play, or other work

topic sentence a sentence stating the main idea of a paragraph, often its first or last sentence

Example

You are preparing to write a term paper about aspects of Japanese culture an American needs to know before visiting or moving to Japan. You go to the library and look in the card catalog or on-line catalog for information on this subject. You find five books that contain material on the subject, so you make a "bibliography card" for each one, giving each source its own number:

①

Everyday Japanese
Edward A. Schwarz and Reiko Ezawa
Passport Books, Lincolnwood, Illinois, 1985
224 pgs.

②

Japan Today!
Theodore F. Welch and Hiroki Kato
Passport Books, Lincolnwood, Illinois, 1989
128 pgs.

③

Japanese Etiquette and Ethics in Business
Boye De Mente
Passport Books, Lincolnwood, Illinois, 1987
192 pgs.

④

The Japanese Influence on America
Boye De Mente
Passport Books, Lincolnwood, Illinois, 1989
192 pgs.

⑤

How to Do Business with the Japanese
Boye DeMente
Passport Books, Lincolnwood, Illinois, 1987
256 pgs.

Then you take notes from each book as you read it, writing just one or two points on each card and making sure to put the source number (from the bibliography card) and the appropriate page number(s) at the top of each card:

①   p. 62

Tel. booths: diff. colors fr. diff. calls: blue = for any dist.; tall red = long dist.; short red = locl.; yellow = espec. good for long dist.

① p. 96

tea cer. very spec. Hosts and guests have spec. formal roles; takes time to learn.

① pp. 128-129

Shinto native religion; means "way of the gods"; no one great fig. of worship; collection of beliefs & ideas abt. proper way of behavior.

①   *pp. 136-139*

Holidays: Respect for the Aged Day; Adults'
Day; Children's Day; Culture Day; Labor
Thanksgiving Day; Dolls' Festival; Girls'
Festival; Boys' Fest.; Fest. of the Weaver; a
day of the children of 3, 5, 7 (Girls 3 & 7, boys
5 taken to shrines. Everyone prays for
their continued health.)

①   *p. 156*

Always leave shoes outside. No shoes
in Jap. house. No slippers in tatami
room. (Tatami mats typ. floor.) Guest
of honor given special seat in front
of takonoma or alcove.

①   p. 162

Visa needed. Visitors must carry passports
all time. 16 diff. statuses for visit. Jap.
Let. of guarantee req. by foreigners who
want to stay long time. Should be
prepared by Jap. ind. or organ. who will
promise to assist foreigner if has
financial or other prob. Students need
special visa to prove actively engaged
in study.

①   p. 166

Jap. room size measured by # of
tatami mats in them.

①   *p. 166*

Flush toilets not taken for granted when buying or renting house.

①   *p. 166*

"Thank you" money paid to landlord non-refund. Very expensive move to Jap. 1 or 2 mos. rent + security dep. + "thank you" money when move in.

②   p. 11

Communal baths. Wash first. One is
clean before entering bathtub in hotel
or home.

②   p. 28

Educ. 6-3-3-4 system: 6 yrs. elem.; 3 yrs.
mid. sch.; 3 hgh sch.; 4 col. 1st 9 yrs.
free & compulsory. Juku, or supp.
schools, help to prepare for col. entr.
tests.

③   p. 22

Vertical society - superior/subordinate relationships; ranking.

③   p. 37

"Wa" or "circle" - mutual trust bet. manager & labor. Loyalty, mutual respons., job security, no competitive pressure; collective resp. for decisions & results. No fool. arnd in workplace.

③   p. 44

Westerners easy to get to know early but not deeply. Jap. take longer to know but are more vulnerable.

③   p. 27

Name cards tell rank. Bilingual name cards handed Jap. side up, presented with both hands and light bow. Can see person's rank on card, estab. vertic. order, language to be used. Really a ceremony.

④   p. 157

Still a lot of arranged marriages in
Jap. Mar. services provided by many
large cos. Jap. males at 30 pressured by
large cos. to marry. Serious handicap
to promotion if not married.

④   p. 161

School 240 days of yr. Amer. Occup. in
1945 elim. "shushin" or "moral educ."
Jap. believe "success in life dtermined
by academic achievement and respect
for rights of others."

④   p. 139

Shoes not worn inside for sanitary reas. Would bring dust and dirt & get on mats. Spec. alcove where shoes kept when not used.

④   p. 141

Sleep on futons. Roll up & put away when fin. sleep.

④   pp. 148-149

Dining cust.: (a) rest. give wet cloths when sit down; hot in winter, cold in sum. (b) Jap. tip in advance. Expect good service. Tips not to employees but to rest. or hotel to defray cost of benefits to employees. (c) Guests at party expected to be part of entertainment.

⑤   p. 249

No place on Jap. lic. for hair or eye color.

⑤   p. 149

In offices & in homes, where seated
spells rank. Nearest door, lowest
rank. Farthest from door in office,
highest rank.

⑤   p. 239

Amer. wives w/out Jap. lang. find
diff. to adjust; husbands entertain, wives
traditionally not incl. Very exp. live
there. Children have easy access to
alcohol.

⑤ p.248

Very expensive own private car. Have to take many tests before can get lic., incl. mechanics test to demonstrate know. of engine and how to make repairs.

⑤ p.249

To get license in Japan, must:
1) attend govt.-reg. course (abt. 6 wks. & $1500) incl.
   a) 25 hrs. class lect. & 5 hrs. on construction & oper. of veh.
   b) practice dry runs on simulator
   c) take 17 sessions on driving range w/ instructor
2) get learner's permit so can then
   a) drive on selected roads and streets
   b) have 10 hrs. off-range driv. in designated areas.

⑤   p. 249

Drive on left side in Jap.

⑤   p. 255

Jap. mix bus. & pleas. Men away from home a lot. Don't entertain at home as Amer. do.

⑤   p. 257

Psychological problems facing for. – tremend. crowded: narrow, winding sts. w/out sidewalks outside major cities. For. res. in Jap. aware of being outsiders.

⑤   p. 102

Bus. done differently. Jap. sit back and wait; Amer. put all on table, unnerved by "inscrutable Orientals." Jap. shrewd negotiators.

See Appendix B for an example showing how the notes taken from these sources can be combined to make a smooth paper.

Procedure ▼

1. When you are taking notes from more than one source for a term paper or research paper, it's a good idea to use index cards instead of notebook paper so you can rearrange your information easily before you begin writing the paper.

2. Each time you read from a different source, make a "bibliography card" that tells

    • the name of the book or magazine you are taking the information from,

    • the author(s),

    • the name and city of the publisher,

    • the year of publication, and

    • the pages you read. (If you read the entire book, write the number of pages in the book.)

    A bibliography card might look like this:

①	**source number**
Everyday Japanese	**book title**
Edward A. Schwartz and Reiko Ezawa	**author**
Passport Books, Lincolnwood, Illinois, 1985	**publisher, city, state, publication date**
224 pgs.	**pages read (pages in book)**

Notice the source number printed and circled at the top of the card. Give every source you use a different number.

3. Take notes as you read each book or article, writing just one or two points on each index card. Put the number of the source you're using (from the bibliography card) and the appropriate page number(s) at the top of each note card:

> ①   *p. 72*
>
> *Students not allowed to wear shorts to school at beginning of 20th cent.*

4. Write your notes in your own words, using abbreviations to save time. If you *do* copy a sentence or two exactly from the source, be sure to put quotation marks around the exact words. Check to make sure you've written the page number where you found the quote at the top of the card. You will need this information when you write your paper.

5. When you have finished your research, find a place where you can lay out all your note cards. Put the cards in groups according to the information on them; for example, all the cards about American schools in one pile and all the cards about French schools in another pile. Then put the sentences from your cards in an order that makes sense to you. It's easy to arrange and rearrange your ideas and information when you're working with index cards.

6. After you have all your notes in order, you can begin to write your paper. See "Writing a Term/Research Paper," pages 158–163, for how to continue the process.

7. Save your bibliography cards to use in footnoting and making a bibliography. See the next chapter on "Writing a Bibliography."

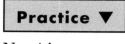

Now it's your turn.

Task: to take notes from several sources for a research paper

Situation: You are preparing to write a research paper on holidays in the United States and how they are celebrated. Go to the library and find at least four sources with information on this topic. Take notes from each source.

Now look back at your notes. Did you remember to:

- make bibliography cards with the titles, authors, and other information about your sources?

- number the bibliography cards and the cards you took notes on so you can match them easily?

- put the information in your own words, using abbreviations and your own shorthand?

- write down only information that relates to your subject, "Holidays in the United States and How They Are Celebrated"?

- write only one or two sentences on each card?

If so, you're ready for the next two chapters of this book!

15 | Academic Writing

Writing a Bibliography

*B*ibliography is a long word, but it has a very simple meaning and purpose. A bibliography is a list of the sources of information used to write a term paper, a research paper, an essay, or to prepare for a debate on a particular subject. For each source, a bibliography tells the author and title of the material, who published the material, where and when it was published, and the page numbers on which the material appears. A bibliography usually appears at the end of a long paper or book.

Rationale

If you have written a paper that includes information, facts, or opinions taken from various sources, you should include a bibliography so that readers of your paper can go to your sources for a variety of reasons:

- Your paper may make them want to read more on the subject because they find it so interesting.

- They may want to read for themselves exactly what a particular source says to see if you have expressed the information completely and correctly.

- They may challenge what you have written. If you give them your sources of information, they can see for themselves that you expressed the information correctly.

- They may want to see how much reading and research you did before writing the paper.

In addition, it's important to give credit to the people whose ideas and information you used. A bibliography is one way to do this.

Materials Needed

bibliography cards listing the author, title, publisher, date and place of publication, and page numbers for each of your sources (see previous chapter on "Taking Notes from Multiple Sources"); typewriter or word processor, unlined paper, model entries for a bibliography

Skills Involved

gathering information; organizing material; alphabetizing; proofreading; typing or word processing

Important Vocabulary

alphabetizing putting words in alphabetical order (words starting with *a* first, words starting with *b* next, etc.)

bibliography a list of sources appearing at the end of a book, article, research paper, or other reading. It tells the title, author, publisher, publication date, and page numbers for each source

challenge question the truth of something

emigration leaving one country to live in another country. (An *emigrant* from one country is an *immigrant* in the country he or she moves to.)

express show feelings or thoughts in words

organize put things in order

publication date for a book, the year it was printed; for a magazine, the date (month/day/year) of the issue

publisher a company that prepares, prints, and sells books, magazines, or other written materials

research looking for and reading information from many sources about a particular topic

source a person, place, or object that contains information

title the name of a book, speech, play, or other work

Example

BIBLIOGRAPHY

Baron, Bruce, Christine Baron, and Bonnie MacDonald. <u>What Did You Learn in School Today?</u> New York: Warner Books, Inc., 1983.

<u>The Chicago Manual of Style</u>. 13th ed. Chicago: The University of Chicago Press, 1982.

Collier, Herbert L. <u>How to Help Your Child Get Better Grades</u>. New York: Pinnacle Books, 1981.

Glasser, William. <u>Schools without Failure</u>. New York: Harper and Row, 1969.

Maculaitis, Jean, and Mona Scheraga. <u>The Complete ESL/EFL Resource Book</u>. Lincolnwood, IL: National Textbook Co., 1988.

Maggs, Margaret Martin. <u>Building Vocabulary</u>, Vol. A, B, C. Lincolnwood, IL: National Textbook Co., 1981.

————. <u>English Across the Curriculum</u>, Vol. 1, 2, 3. Lincolnwood, IL: National Textbook Co., 1983.

Murphey, Tim. "Teaching for Peak Relevance Using International Pop Music." <u>TESOL Newsletter</u> 19.6 (December 1985): 13.

Procedure ▼

1. The bibliography for a paper or book should contain information about every source the author used in writing the paper or book. As you do your research, keep a record of the sources you use by making a bibliography card for each one. (See the previous chapter, "Taking Notes from Multiple Sources," for directions on how to make bibliography cards.)

2. Proofread your cards. Be sure you have the correct spellings, dates, and other information for each source.

3. When you have finished writing your paper, put the bibliography cards for the sources you actually used in alphabetical order according to the last names of the authors.

4. Make a practice copy of your bibliography. Write or type BIBLIOGRAPHY at the top of the page in the center. Make an entry for each source, following the formats given below and in the Example for various types of sources. Be sure the entries are in alphabetical order. Look at the Example for help.

5.   Follow this format to make an entry for a book:

a.   Put the author's last name first, followed by a comma and his or her first name. Put a period after the author's first name. Then type the title of the book and underline it. Put a period after the title.

Blosser, Betsy. <u>Living in English.</u>

b.   Next, put the publisher's city and state. It's all right to abbreviate the name of the state. Separate the city from the state with a comma. Put a colon after the state.

Lincolnwood, IL:

c.   Type the name of the publisher and the date of publication next. Use a comma to separate the publisher from the date of publication. Put a period after the publication date. That is the end of the entry.

National Textbook Co., 1989.

d.   If the book has more than one author, list the authors' names in the order they appear in the book. Follow these formats:

Jones, Kate, and Elizabeth Grimm.

Casey, Robert, J. D. Thompson, and Paula Locke.

DeMar, Letitia, et al.

e. If no author is given for the book, start the entry with the title and alphabetize it by the first word (other than *a*, *an*, or *the*) in the title.

6. Follow this format to make an entry for a magazine or journal article:

a. Put the author's last name first, followed by a comma and his or her first name. Put a period after the author's first name. Then type the title of the article and put a period after it. Put quotation marks before and after the title.

Runnels, Curtis. "Greece Before the Greeks: The Neanderthals and Their Fate."

b. Type the name of the magazine or journal and underline it. Then put the volume number of the issue the article appeared in. If there's an issue number too, put a period after the volume number and add the issue number.

Archaeology 42

TESOL Quarterly 22.4

c. Next, put the publication date in parentheses. Then put a colon followed by the page number(s)on which the article appeared. Put a period after the page number(s). This is the end of the entry.

(March/April 1989): 43–47.

d. If the article has more than one author, list the authors' names as shown in step 5(d) on page 152.

e. If no author is given for the article, start the entry with the title and alphabetize it by the first word (other than *a*, *an*, or *the*) in the title.

7. If you have more than one book or article by the same author(s) to list in your bibliography, put them in alphabetical order by title. You can save time and space by replacing the author's name with three hyphens in each entry after the first one.

Raudsepp, Eugene. How Creative Are You? New York: The Putnam Publishing Group, 1981.
———. More Creative Growth Games. New York: The Putnam Publishing Group, 1980.

8. If you need to make an entry for a source other than a book or a magazine or journal article, refer to a stylebook such as the *MLA Handbook for Writers of Research Papers*, fourth edition, by Joseph Gibaldi (New York: The Modern Language Association of America, 1995). The *MLA Handbook* contains detailed instructions and examples of bibliography entries for many different types of sources.

9. Proofread your bibliography. Then type a final copy and proofread it.

10. Put your bibliography at the end of your paper. It should be the last page of your work.

Practice ▼

Now it's your turn.

Task: to write a bibliography

Situation: You have been asked to write a paper about emigration laws. The first thing you have to do is read what the emigration laws are for different countries. Since you are going to do the bibliography only, and will not actually write the paper now, choose three or four countries whose emigration laws interest you. Go to the library and look for sources that tell about the emigration laws of these countries. Remember to take index cards with you so you can make a bibliography card for each source you find. Prepare a bibliography of at least four books and/or articles on this subject.

Did you remember to

- put your sources in alphabetical order?

- include all the necessary information? (See Procedure.)

- use the correct punctuation?

- type or write your bibliography on unlined paper?

- proofread?

16 Academic Writing

Writing a Term/ Research Paper

Some high school teachers and most college professors ask students to write at least one long paper for each of their classes. Students are usually given several weeks or even months to work on these papers. They're not hard to do, and they can be very interesting for the writer as well as for the reader. Research papers take time and care, but with the right attitude and materials, you can learn a great deal and earn a grade to be proud of.

Rationale

Writing a term paper or research paper will give you practice in developing many skills and will help you learn more about a certain topic. Because of the limited time available in the classroom, teachers can't always teach as much as they would like about every subject. If you research a topic on your own, you will learn about the subject in more depth. Also, your *active* participation in the learning process will help you remember what you've learned.

Materials Needed

3" × 5" or larger index cards, pen and pencil, several sources containing information on your topic, typewriter or word processor, unlined paper for typing, composition paper

Skills Involved

locating sources; gathering information; recognizing important material; taking and organizing notes; using correct grammar, punctuation, and spelling; writing sentences and paragraphs in an interesting and organized way; using footnotes; creating a bibliography

If you are asked to choose your own topic, another very important skill you will learn is how to narrow a topic to one that is appropriate for a term paper.

Important Vocabulary

appropriate right, suitable

attitude a way of feeling or behaving

author writer

bibliography a list of sources appearing at the end of a book, article, research paper, or other reading. It tells the title, author, publisher, publication date, and page numbers for each source.

footnote a note usually placed at the bottom of a page to explain or give more information about something on the page, such as the source of the material. When you see a raised number at the end of a sentence, you should look at the bottom of the page for a *footnote*.

footnoting making a footnote, often to tell the source of an idea or fact

index cards small, usually white cards, often lined on one side and unlined on the other. The most common size is 3" × 5" (three inches by five inches)

in more depth in more detail, more thoroughly

limited kept to a certain area or amount, restricted

narrow a topic focus on a specific part of a topic

organizing putting things in order

publisher a company that prepares, prints, and sells books, magazines, or other written materials

research looking for and reading information from many sources about a particular topic

research paper a paper of several pages that usually deals with one subject in depth and is based on information gathered through research

source a person, place, or object from which information is obtained

taking notes writing down in abbreviated form what you want to remember from something you're reading or hearing

term paper a paper on a particular subject, usually due near the end of a school term. A term paper usually requires research, footnotes and a bibliography.

title the name of a book, speech, play, or other work

topic subject

Example

See Appendix C for a sample term paper.

Procedure ▼

1. Choose a topic and narrow it down to something realistic. You don't want your topic to be too general. For example, entire books have been written about the lives of famous people. If you want to write a term paper about a famous person, you will have to narrow your topic by focusing on one part of that person's life. If you want to write about the effects of war on people's lives, you will have to choose certain wars and the people and countries who were affected by them, rather than trying to write about all wars. Otherwise, your information would be too general and your paper would be too long. Your topic should give you an idea for a title for the paper.

2. Go to the library and use the vertical files, card catalog or on-line catalog, and *Reader's Guide to Periodical Literature*, to find sources for your paper.

3. Take notes as you read each source, following the procedure described in the chapter on "Taking Notes from Multiple Sources," pages 122–148.

4. When all your notes are written on index cards, group them by putting together the cards from different sources that contain information about the same subject. For example, if you are writing about the way teenagers dressed in the 1950s, you might put all your cards about hairstyles in different parts of the world in one pile, all your cards about leather jackets in another pile, etc. Or you might group your cards by country, so you could talk about the styles in one country at a time. Since your notes are on individual cards, they are easy to work with. The important thing is to organize them so they will make sense to the reader.

5. Make an outline for your paper, following the directions on pages 82–92.

6. Write an introduction for your paper. The introduction is the first part of a paper. It tells what the purpose of your paper is—why you are writing on this particular subject. It leads the reader into the information you have put together from your notes.

An introduction for a paper on the history and development of the short story, for example, might be something like this:

Short Stories and You[1]

For as long as there have been people, there have been stories about people. From our earliest beginnings, human beings have been curious about each other and have satisfied that curiosity with myths, legends, adventure tales, fantasy—stories. People respond to stories that have a special enduring quality—a sparkle of life, a bit of truth, a glimpse of ourselves.

7.   After you have written your introduction, go back to your note cards and make sure you've organized them well. Write your paper, working with your cards in order and adding sentences that will make your paper interesting and easy to understand. This will be a *rough draft* or *practice copy* that you can read and correct and rewrite until you've expressed everything as well as you can.

8.   As you write your paper, be sure to tell where you got the information you are using. One way to do this is by footnoting. In general, you should make a footnote for each piece of information you use that is not common knowledge.

A footnote tells the name and author of the source in which you found a piece of information, plus all the other information a bibliography entry for that source would include. (See pages 149–158.) A footnote also tells the page on which the information appears in the book or article. Below are examples of the format you should follow when making a footnote for a book or magazine article.

[1]Betsy J. Blosser, Living in English Lincolnwood, IL: National Textbook Co., —— **book**
1989. 122.
[2]Charles E. Cobb, Jr., "Living with Radiation," National Geographic 175.4 —— **magazine article**
(April 1989): 411–12.

[1]John S. Simmons and Malcolm E. Stern, *The Short Story and You* Lincolnwood, IL: National Textbook Co., 1986. vii.

As you write your paper, whenever you include a piece of information that is not common knowledge—and *especially* when you use a direct quote from someone else—put a raised number at the end of the sentence containing that information. Then, at the bottom of the page, make a footnote with the same number that tells where you got the information. Number the first footnote in your paper number one, and continue numbering your footnotes in order throughout your paper.

If you prefer, and if your teacher permits, you can use endnotes in your paper instead of footnotes. Endnotes contain the same information, follow the same format, and are numbered the same way as footnotes. The only difference is that they are placed together at the end of the paper, just before the bibliography, instead of at the bottom of each page. See Appendix C, pages 173–182, for an example.

After you have made one footnote or endnote for a particular source, any additional notes for that same source can be shortened to include only the author's last name and the page or pages on which the information appeared:

[3]Blosser, 74–75.

However, if you are using two or more sources by the same author, you must include the title of the book or article, too:

[4]Blosser, English for Adult Living 39.

For more information and examples of footnotes and endnotes for different types of sources, refer to a stylebook such as the *MLA Handbook for Writers of Research Papers*, fourth edition, by Joseph Gibaldi (New York: The Modern Language Association of America, 1995).

9. Type your paper on unlined paper.

10. Put your bibliography cards in alphabetical order and prepare your bibliography, following the directions in "Writing a Bibliography," pages 149–157.

11.   Type your bibliography and put it at the end of your paper.

12.   Be sure your pages are in order. Number them at the bottom of the page, beginning with page 2.

13.   Create a separate title page for your paper. Be sure it includes the title, your name, class, and the date, as well as any other information your teacher requires. See Appendix C for an example.

14.   Proofread the final copy of your whole paper and correct any mistakes before giving it to your teacher.

Practice ▼

Now it's your turn.

Task: to write a term/research paper

Situation: Your teacher has asked you to write a term paper. You can choose your own topic. Remember to follow the directions in the chapters on "Making an Outline," "Taking Notes from Multiple Sources," and "Writing a Bibliography." You have a lot of work to do; but if you follow the directions, it will be easy and rewarding. Before you begin, reread the list of "Materials Needed" for this chapter. You will need to use your own paper for this Practice.

Appendices

Appendix A

Transcript of Two Lectures

(Transcript of two lectures for use in Procedure and Practice, "Taking Notes from a Lecture." See page 109.)

Procedure lecture

There are several ways in which American dining customs differ from those elsewhere. An invited dinner guest is expected to arrive at the specified time, contrary to customs in some countries. The use of the knife and fork is often different. The fork is used mostly in the right hand. It gathers the food without help from the knife, which is generally used only to cut meat and potatoes, and is to the right of the plate when not in use. And while in many places the napkin (cloth or paper used to clean the lips and hands at the table) is put around the neck, here it is put on the lap (the top part of the legs of a seated person). Finally, Americans tend to eat foods with their fingers. At informal dinners and picnics, chicken, corn-on-the-cob, pizza, and tortillas (a Mexican food) are eaten without utensils (knives, spoons, and forks).[1]

Practice lecture

Do you know how to take a test? When you take a test, you must know the information on the test. You must also know how to take the test. It is important to understand the directions and follow them.

Some tests don't ask you to write information. They ask you to decide if something is correct or not correct. These are often called "true or false" tests. Some tests ask

[1]Jann Huizenga, *Looking at American Food*, Lincolnwood, IL: National Textbook Co., 1987. page 30.

you to decide which answer is correct. You must choose the correct answer from two or three possible answers. These are "multiple choice" tests.

Some tests ask you to put two parts of an answer together. Usually one part of the answer is on the left side of the paper and the other part of the answer is on the right side of the paper. These are "matching" tests. Some tests have sentences with a missing word or words. Sometimes the missing words are listed and you must write them in the correct places. Sometimes there are more words listed than you need, and you must decide which ones to use. Sometimes there are no words listed. Then you must think of the missing words and write them in. These are called "fill-in" tests. Sometimes you have to answer the questions on a test by writing all the information in paragraph form. This is called an "essay test."[2]

[2]Some of the material for this lecture is taken from *English Across the Curriculum 2,* by Margaret Martin Maggs (Lincolnwood, IL: National Textbook Co., 1982) pages 21–28.

Appendix B

Example of a Paper with Notes

(Example of a paper written using notes from many sources. See "Taking Notes from Multiple Sources," page 122.)

AN AMERICAN FAMILY IN JAPAN

Planning to move to Japan? There are many cultural and educational differences you should be aware of to make life easier for you and your family.

If you have children, you should know that the educational system is different in many ways, although the system is divided by years much the same way as it is in the United States. Education is free in Japan the first nine years and is compulsory through ninth grade.[1] Students from other countries need a special visa via a note of authenticity from the school they are attending to verify they are actively engaged in study.[2] This is in addition to the special visa that you will need to come to Japan to live and work. Private schools with American curricula are available in the big cities at high prices.

When the American Occupation took over Japanese schools in 1945, they eliminated <u>shushin</u> or "moral education."[3] The Japanese taught morality based on the Confucian concept that "success in life is determined by academic achievement and respect for the rights of others."

Japanese students attend school for 240 days each year. <u>Juku,</u> or supplementary schools, exist to help students prepare for college entrance tests, which are very difficult.

There are sixteen different statuses for visitors to Japan. Visitors must carry their passports at all times. Visas are needed and a letter of guarantee is required for foreigners who want to stay a long time. This should be prepared by a Japanese individual or organization who will promise to assist the foreigner if he or she has financial or other problems. If you are a foreigner employed in Japan, you must obtain a letter of employment showing the period of employment and how much you will be earning. If you are not employed, you may have to show how you will support yourself.[4]

[1] Theodore F. Welch and Hiroki Kato, <u>Japan Today!</u> Lincolnwood, IL: Passport Books, 1986. 28.

[2] Edward A. Schwarz and Reiko Ezawa. <u>Everyday Japanese</u> Lincolnwood, IL: Passport Books, 1988. 163.

[3] Boye de Mente, <u>The Japanese Influence on America</u> Lincolnwood, IL: Passport Books, 1989. 161.

[4] Schwarz and Ezawa 162.

Business practices are very different in Japan, and many Americans lose "deals" because they don't understand the culture. For example, the American businessman usually tells everything he has to say and expects the Japanese to do the same. The Japanese businessman, on the other hand, will sit back and listen and not say anything, sometimes for a very, very long period of time. The American gets nervous and starts talking too much and making concessions. The more he talks, the quieter the Japanese gets. He is a very shrewd negotiator. He also does little business with women.[5] That is another story.

Japanese society is vertical; it is based on superior/subordinate relationships.[6] When you walk into a Japanese office, you know what rank a person holds by where he or she is sitting. The closer a person sits to the door, the lower his or her rank is. The first introduction between businessmen is not a handshake but the presentation of the Name Card, like our business card, which tells the person's name, rank, and company. Bilingual cards are handed Japanese side up, with both hands and a slight bow. You are treated according to your rank after your card has been presented and read.[7]

Wa, or "circle," stands for the mutual trust between manager and laborer. There is loyalty, mutual responsibility, job security, collective responsibility for decisions and results, and no competitive pressure. There also is no fooling around in the workplace.[8]

The Japanese mix business and pleasure and do a lot of entertaining outside the home. Women are traditionally not included and this makes for some very lonely American wives. If wives do not speak Japanese, they often suffer from feelings of isolation in the tremendously crowded atmosphere where they never can forget they are foreigners.[9] Much time is spent getting their children to and from school since they must provide their own transportation and since driving in Japan is a very different experience. Japanese drive on the left side of the road as people do in England.

[5] Boye De Mente, How to Do Business with the Japanese Lincolnwood, IL: Passport Books, 1987. 101.
[6] Boye De Mente, Japanese Etiquette and Ethics in Business Lincolnwood, IL: Passport Books, 1987. 22.
[7] De Mente, Japanese Etiquette and Ethics in Business 28.
[8] De Mente, Japanese Etiquette and Ethics in Business 28.
[9] De Mente, How to Do Business with the Japanese 239.

If you have a driver's license from the United States, you can get a license in Japan, but if you have to get a license for the first time, that is a time- and money-consuming experience. Before you can get a license, you have to take a mechanics test to prove your knowledge of engines and how to repair them.[10] You must attend a government-regulated driving course that includes five hours on the construction and operation of a motor vehicle as part of twenty-five hours of classroom lectures. You have to practice dry runs on a simulator and have seventeen sessions at the wheel on a driving range with an instructor. Then you receive a learner's permit, which allows you to drive on selected roads and streets. After completing ten hours of off-range driving in designated areas and spending about $1,500 for the course, you can try for your driver's license. There is no place on the license for the color of a person's hair or eyes because Japan is such a homogeneous country.[11]

Finding a place to live in Japan is also an experience for the American. Housing can be very expensive. Besides having to pay one or two months' rent plus a security deposit before moving in, there is also a nonrefundable "thank you money" gift given to the landlord. Flush toilets should not be taken for granted when renting or buying a home. Japanese room size is measured by the number of <u>tatami mats</u> in the room. Tatami mats are the typical floor covering in a Japanese house. As a sanitary measure, shoes are never worn inside the house. They would bring in dust and dirt that would get on the tatami mats. There is a special alcove where shoes are kept when not in use.[12] <u>Futons,</u> bed rolls, are rolled up and put away when they are not in use for sleeping. A guest of honor in the house is always given a special seat in front of the <u>takonoma,</u> an alcove.

Very little entertaining is done in the home. When you go to a restaurant, you are given wet cloths when you sit down—hot in winter, cool in summer. Japanese often tip in advance to ensure good service. Tips are given not to the employees but to the hotel or restaurant to help defray the cost of benefits to the employees. Good service is expected. Tips are not expected by employees and are forbidden in some places. Party participants are expected to be a part of the entertainment during a

[10]De Mente, <u>How to Do Business with the Japanese</u> 248.
[11]De Mente, <u>How to Do Business with the Japanese</u> 249.
[12]De Mente, <u>The Japanese Influence on America</u> 139.

gathering in a restaurant or night club.[13] Below is some other interesting general and cultural information for the non-Japanese:

Communal baths are still a part of Japanese life. However, people are expected to wash before they get into the tub, whether at home or at a hotel. One is expected to be clean when entering a communal tub, where the water is not changed with each group of bathers.[14] There are still a lot of arranged marriages in Japan. Marriage services are provided by many large companies. Japanese males at age thirty are pressured to marry by the companies they work for. Being single is a serious handicap to promotion.[15]

The Japanese celebrate many holidays we don't celebrate here; for example, Respect for the Aged Day, Adults' Day, Children's Day, Culture Day, Labor Thanksgiving Day, Dolls' Festival, Girls' and Boys' Festivals, Festival of the Weaver, and many others. Japanese send New Year's cards the way we send Christmas cards. January 15 is set aside to honor the twenty-five year old: it is the day of legally becoming an adult.

Shinto is the indigenous religion of Japan. The word means "way of the gods." There is no one great figure of worship but rather a collection of beliefs and ideas about the proper ways of behavior that have developed over two thousand years.[16] The tea ceremony is very special. The host and guests have special formal roles. The ceremony takes time to learn. For example, pocket paper is used by guests to place wagashi or Japanese cake on, or to wipe the tea bowl dry after drinking tea.[17]

Finally, knowing something about Japanese telephone booths can really help. There are different colors for different calls. Blue is for any distance; tall red booths are for long distance; short red booths are for local calls; and yellow booths are especially good for long distance.[18]

There are many good books to read on the life and culture of Japan. We suggest those in the bibliography as a good start.

[13]De Mente, The Japanese Influence on America 148–149.
[14]Welch and Kato 11.
[15]De Mente, The Japanese Influence on America 157.
[16]Schwarz and Ezawa 128–129
[17]Schwarz and Ezawa 96.
[18]Schwarz and Ezawa 62.

Appendix C

Example of a Term Paper

(Example of a term paper. See "Writing a Term/Research Paper," page 158.)

THE AMISH
By Kathy Blattner
Richwoods High School

Even though we live in a highly technological society, there is a group of people who live successfully resistant to change, modern conveniences, fads, world crisis, or social status. This group is the Amish.[1]

In 1693 in Europe, Jacob Ammann led a group of people to form a group separate from the Mennonites. The group became the Amish, taking their name from their leader.[2] The Amish are a plain religious group that has maintained many of the same beliefs as the Mennonites, although the Amish do follow their beliefs more strictly.[3]

The Amish wanted to come to America to escape from the persecution they suffered in Europe. While in Europe, they were not allowed to buy or even rent land; and they were often heavily taxed. They were not allowed to live together in a community and therefore were unable to be a close group.[4]

The Amish began to come to America early in the 1700s. Within one hundred years, they were almost nonexistent in Europe, having either left or merged again with Mennonite churches. An invitation from William Penn to the Amish brought many to the colony of Pennsylvania. Soon they spread to other areas of the new country and established communities and congregations.[5]

In their early years in Europe, the Amish were persecuted for their beliefs. As a result, they held their church services in homes. Every other Sunday, the Amish still meet for worship in the home of one of the congregation.[6] Only the members of the congregation know whose home the service will be in.[7] They sit on hard benches that are moved from house to house. Their homes are designed to hold the congregation by opening up smaller rooms to make one large room.[8] The sermon, worship, and singing of hymns are done in German,[9] and might last from three to four hours.[10] Following the worship service, dinner is enjoyed by the entire group.[11]

A special congregational meeting called an Ordnungsgemee is held twice a year to make the rules that become the Ordnung. These rules set down the way an Amish person lives. All members of the congregation know the Ordnung. The older rules of the Ordnung have been printed. These rules apply mainly to the principles of separation, apostasy, nonresistance, and exclusion. It is usually the borderline issues that are discussed by the congregation at the meeting. The issues of contemporary nature and those that apply only to a specific congregation continue to be unwritten.[12]

The Ordnung clarifies what is sinful or worldly. Many of the rules are based on Biblical passages; however, some have no Biblical support. These rules are justified by saying that it would be worldly to do otherwise. It is important for the Amish to maintain their separation from the world, and the congregation must agree on how to remain separate. The meetings held twice a year provide time for the members to declare their unity toward issues.[13]

Excommunication from the church is the punishment given an Amish person accused of disobeying the Ordnung. The offender is warned and is expelled only after he refuses to change. The wrong behavior may be living openly in sin, causing divisions among the Amish, or teaching false doctrines. Specific examples of wrong behavior that could lead to excommunication are buying a car, talking to an excommunicated person, disobeying the dress code, or arguing with another person.[14]

When an Amish person is expelled from the church, the Ordnung calls for the congregation to practice Meidung. This is a shunning and calls for avoiding association with the excommunicated person.[15] "The Biblical instruction is that one neither 'eat' with such a person nor 'keep company' (I Cor. 5:11)."[16]

A person may be pardoned and become part of the congregation once again if he acknowledges his sins and makes amends. If it is a minor offense, he needs to make only a formal apology to the church. However, if the offense is major, he needs to have the welcome of the bishop after confessing to the wrong on his knees. The fear of being shunned by their family and friends keeps some Amish from disobeying the Ordnung.[17]

An Amish person is not born Amish. All men and women must decide themselves if they want to become Amish. If they do, they are baptized into the church.[18] The vow of baptism is an expression of faith, so it can be given only to those old enough to understand and pledge their faith.[19] They realize that to become Amish means to live by the rules of the church. This affects the entire life style of a person since religion and everyday life are intertwined.[20]

A very special occasion in the life of the Amish is the birth of a child. Each child born into an Amish family is felt to be a gift of God.[21] Amish children are a very important part of the community. No child is ever unwelcome. A newborn child brings happiness to the family and community since he will enlarge their Amish society. Children also mean more church members and workers.[22]

For the first two years of an Amish child's life, he is given everything he wants. After that, the parents begin to discipline the child.[23] Children receive "on-the-spot" discipline from their relatives because they work closely and almost continuously together.[24] An Amish child will soon learn that he is "different" from "English" children, but he will learn to take pride in his differences and follow his parents' example. Children are raised with such great amounts of love and care that they never feel secure outside their community.[25]

Marriage in an Amish community means that a couple is ready to move from youth and adolescence to adulthood. Courting is kept secret. The majority of the community will not know of an intended wedding until it is announced in church. Close friends of a potential bride or groom often look for signs of an upcoming wedding. An overabundance of celery growing in the garden of the potential bride is considered a sign, since large amounts of celery are used at weddings. When the father of a potential bridegroom tries to buy extra land, it is also considered a sign of an upcoming wedding. When a young man is ready to be married, he tells his minister, and the minister talks to the bridegroom's intended fiancée. He verifies her wish to be married and obtains the consent of her parents. The intent of the couple to be married is later announced or "published" during a church service.[26]

Another major occurrence in the lives of the Amish, although not as happy as marriage, is death. Death is a natural part of life to the Amish. The Amish live to "store treasures" in heaven instead of accumulating material goods. The relatives do grieve, but they do not have a long period of mourning. Remembering the person and his role in life is emphasized. The process of preparing for a funeral is a community project. Someone makes the coffin when it is needed, and the burial site is prepared while the family and friends prepare the body. Some communities have bodies embalmed, although many do not. The tasks of running the home and farm are taken over by friends until the funeral is over. There is no payment to anyone for services. The body is usually kept in the home and someone sits with the dead day and night. The funeral is held on the third day after death. The theme is usually centered around the Biblical theme, "The Lord giveth and the Lord taketh away." The cemetery is small and people are not buried in family plots but in the order they die. The marker is made by another community member and gives only the name and dates of birth and death.[27]

The simplicity shown in handling the death and funeral of an Amish person is also shown in their homes. They are very plain and simple and there are no decorative items. There may be a few plants and a calendar, but no pictures, mirrors, or knickknacks are allowed. The Amish must not use electrical appliances or bottled gas, and they are not allowed to have radios. These rules have been the same for years.[28]

The clothing worn by the Amish has also been the same style for years. Plainness and simplicity are important so no one looks or feels different from anyone else.[29] There may be slight differences in the way an Amish person dresses in separate Amish communities. These differences may seem small to an outsider, but they mean a lot to an Amish person.[30]

Amish women wear dresses that are completely alike. The dress pattern that they use has been handed down through the generations. Their dresses can be any solid color, but most women choose black, blue, green, or tan. A married woman always wears an apron that is either black or matches the color of her dress. An unmarried woman always wears a white apron.[31] Little girls' dresses may have bright colors but may not have any pattern in the fabric.[32] Amish women must wear their "prayer caps" at all times. The caps are made of starched white organdy. They are worn on the back of their heads, and are tied under their chins in a small, neat bow.[33]

The clothing worn by men must not have buttons because decorations of any kind on clothing are rejected entirely by Amish custom.[34] Also, since the Amish are pacifists, buttons are not used on clothing because they were originally used on military uniforms.[35] Men's hats are black and are made with specific regulations as to the size of the brim and the crown.[36] In most Amish communities, men are not allowed to wear neckties because they do not serve a useful purpose. A few communities, however, have allowed a narrow, black ribbon bow to be worn to church services and other dressy occasions.[37]

Just as the Amish have a uniformity in dress, they also have a uniform love and concern for one another. They provide support in times of trouble, so they do not need insurance coverage. In case of fire, the entire community will help rebuild the lost house or barn, contributing both materials and physical labor.[38] Although a community "barn-raising" becomes a social event, it is not planned as one. The Amish feel secure in knowing that in times of trouble, the other members of the church will help them. The spirit of fun and fellowship is always in the air at community gatherings. These feelings of security help the Amish in their daily work.[39]

The Amish farmer feels that the Bible tells him his job is to replenish the earth, till the soil, and have an abundant harvest. He loves the soil and works with it with care.[40] The farmer is not concerned with the highest possible yield per acre. He is mainly growing food for his family to eat, as well as feed for his animals. He is also concerned with preserving the soil, which he feels is a gift from God.[41] Rules governing farming are a part of the Ordnung also. In most Amish communities, all of the farm equipment must be horse-drawn.[42] One advantage for the farmer when using horses rather than a tractor is his ability to hear and observe the wildlife around him.[43]

Even though most Amish men are farmers, each community has some businessmen who make the items necessary for use in homes and farming. There are those who make buggies, caskets, farm machinery, and household furniture.[44] Some shops needed by an Amish community are a blacksmith and a harness shop.[45] The Amish are the major manufacturers of buggies, which are very expensive.[46]

Before joining their chosen trade or profession, each Amish girl and boy attends school for eight years. They attend one-room schools with all grades together, and their teacher probably has only an eighth-grade education herself if she is Amish. Some states are demanding that the teachers be certified; therefore, the teacher may be non-Amish in some communities. The Amish are struggling with this change forced on them and are forming Amish parochial school programs. It is considered unnecessary and worldly for a student to go to high school. Instead, the girls are taught to care for a home, and the boys are taught the basics of farm management.[47]

Although the Amish do not have modern conveniences to help them with their daily work, their lives are not dull. Visiting friends and attending auctions are just two of the things that the Amish do to keep busy. Sewing and quilting provide a chance for the women to talk, and even the big job of harvesting is fun when a lot of friends work together.[48]

Children also have many ways of having fun after they have finished their chores. They have homemade toys, and they enjoy many games.[49] Popping corn and pulling taffy are just two of the things that Amish children and teenagers do at "sings." They also provide the older boys with the chance to take their favorite girls home in their "courting buggies."[50] A favorite game among Amish men is chess. They often will even play against "English" (non-Amish) players. They are not, however, allowed to play cards.[51]

Although the Amish do not have much vacation time, visiting natural sites like the Grand Canyon and going to zoos are accepted since they are visiting gifts from God.[52]

One family took their children to St. Louis and while there visited Forest Park Zoo. In commenting on the trip, the mother was amused, saying that her family proved to be about as much of an attraction at the zoo as the animals.[53]

The enjoyment of a Sunday afternoon drive is done in a horse-drawn buggy, since another modern convenience rejected by the Amish is the automobile. An unmarried man is apt to drive a one-seated buggy, while a family will have a two-seated one. One false belief most people have about the Amish is that they do not travel very often. The fact that the Amish have horses and buggies rather than automobiles does not keep them from traveling. Some Amish will hire a driver and his car to take them to a distant town for shopping. If most of the community is planning to go, someone may charter a bus. Each family will bring enough food to last them until they arrive at their destination. If they are going to be traveling for several days, they will stop at Amish communities along the way. At these communities, they will be fed and can spend the night. The Amish can travel all over the United States and never have to buy a meal or pay for a hotel.[54] "One Amishman, commenting on this practice, chuckled and said, 'We call that Mennoniting around!'"[55]

Very few Amish leave the faith. The closeness felt among the community members provides a bond that few want to break.[56] "Only about five per cent of the Amish break away."[57] The number of Amish in the United States has increased some over the years. This may seem strange since intermarriage is rare and seeking converts is not widely practiced. The reason for the increase would seem to come mainly from the common practice of having large families of seven or more children. The children continue to abide by the traditions of generations before them.[58]

Although the Amish are separate from the rest of the world, they do not need to completely isolate themselves to remain stable. They do business in nearby non-Amish communities by trading their goods for items at stores. They are also allowed to seek medical care and other professional services.[59]

The Amish take pleasure in the simple things in their lives. Their interests in their homes, their community, their neighbors, and their hobbies keep them content.[60] The strongest bond that holds the Amish people together is their faith. Their belief that God has a personal interest in each life and each home and each community ties them tightly together.[61]

It has been over 275 years since the Amish first settled in America, but their customs and style of living have remained nearly the same.[62] As one Amish farmer said, "It is a satisfying life, not for everyone perhaps, but certainly for us."[63]

ENDNOTES

[1] James A. Warner and Donald M. Denlinger, <u>The Gentle People</u> Soudersburg, PA: Mill Bridge Museum, 1969. 12–13.

[2] Philip Shriver Klein and Ari Hoogenboom, <u>A History of Pennsylvania</u> New York: McGraw-Hill, Inc., 1973. 206.

[3] Millen Brand, <u>Fields of Peace</u> Garden City, NY: Doubleday and Company, Inc., 1970. 32.

[4] Elmer Schwieder and Dorothy Schwieder, <u>A Peculiar People: Iowa's Old Order Amish</u> Ames: The Iowa State University Press, 1975. 14–15.

[5] Schwieder and Schwieder 9, 16.

[6] Klein and Hoogenboom 441.

[7] John M. Zielinski, "The Amish in Illinois," <u>Adventure Road</u> 14 (September 1978): 16–17.

[8] Brand 63.

[9] Klein and Hoogenboom 441.

[10] <u>The Ohio Guide</u> New York: Oxford University Press, 1948. 394.

[11] Klein and Hoogenboom 441.

[12] John A. Hostetler, <u>Amish Society</u> Baltimore: Johns Hopkins University Press, 1980. 84–85.

[13] Hostetler 84–85.

[14] Hostetler 86–89.

[15] Hostetler 86–89.

[16] Hostetler 86–89.

[17] Hostetler 86–89.

[18] Marc A. Olshan, "Should We Live Like the Amish?" <u>Christianity Today</u> 27 (February 4, 1983): 68.

[19] <u>The Ohio Guide</u> 394.

[20] Olshan 68.

[21] Warner and Denlinger 90.

[22] Hostetler 157.

[23] Hostetler 157–158.

[24] Merle Good and Phyllis Good, <u>20 Most Asked Questions About the Amish and Mennonites</u> Lancaster: Good Books, 1979. 57.

[25] Hostetler 157–158.

[26] Hostetler 191–192.

[27] Schwieder and Schwieder 34–35.

[28] Brand 63, 68.

[29] Brand 63.

[30] Hostetler 234–235.

[31] Elmer L. Smith, <u>The Amish</u> Lebanon, PA: Applied Arts Publishers, 1973. 25.

[32] Brand 63.

[33] Smith 25.

[34] Brand 63–64.

[35] Warner and Denlinger 12.

[36] Brand 63–64.

[37] Smith 25.

[38] Brand 62.

[39] Smith 27.

[40] Warner and Denlinger 133.

[41] David Kline, "Amish Farming: The Gentle Way of Life," <u>Saturday Evening Post</u> 255 (March 1983): 62–63.

[42] Warner and Denlinger 108.

[43] Kline 62–63.

[44] <u>The Ohio Guide</u> 394–395.

[45] Paul M. Angle, ed. <u>Illinois Guide and Gazetteer</u> Chicago: Rand McNally and Company, 1969. 62.

[46] Brand 68, 71.

[47] Warner and Denlinger 44–45.

[48] Zielinski 17.

[49] Brand 58.

[50] Zielinski 17.

[51] Brand 58, 68.

[52] Schwieder and Schwieder 71–72.

[53] Schwieder and Schwieder 71–72.

[54] Schwieder and Schwieder 71–72.

[55] Schwieder and Schwieder 71–72.

[56] Brand 71.

[57] Brand 71.

58 Klein and Hoogenboom 441.

59 Schwieder and Schwieder 68–69.

60 Cornelius Weygandt, <u>The Plenty of Pennsylvania</u> New York: H. C. Kinsey and Company, Inc., 1942. 84.

61 Good and Good 82.

62 Warner and Denlinger 12–13.

63 Kline 63.

BIBLIOGRAPHY

Angle, Paul M., ed. <u>Illinois Guide and Gazetteer</u>. Chicago: Rand McNally and Company, 1969.

Branden, Millen. <u>Fields of Peace</u>. Garden City, NY: Doubleday and Company, Inc., 1970.

Good, Merle, and Phyllis Good. <u>20 Most Asked Questions About the Amish and Mennonites</u>. Lancaster: Good Books, 1979.

Hostetler, John A. <u>Amish Society</u>. Baltimore: Johns Hopkins University Press, 1980.

Klein, Philip Shriver, and Ari Hoogenboom. <u>A History of Pennsylvania</u>. New York: McGraw-Hill, Inc., 1973.

Kline, David. "Amish Farming: The Gentle Way of Life." <u>Saturday Evening Post</u> 255 (March 1983): 62–63.

<u>The Ohio Guide</u>. Compiled by workers of the Writers' Program. New York: Oxford University Press, 1948.

Olshan, Marc A. "Should We Live Like the Amish?" <u>Christianity Today</u> 27 (February 4, 1983): 68.

Schwieder, Elmer, and Dorothy Schwieder. <u>A Peculiar People: Iowa's Old Order Amish</u>. Ames: The Iowa State University Press, 1975.

Smith, Elmer L. <u>The Amish</u>. Lebanon, PA: Applied Arts Publishers, 1973.

Warner, James A., and Donald M. Denlinger. <u>The Gentle People</u>. Soudersburg, PA: Mill Bridge Museum, 1969.

Weygandt, Cornelius. <u>The Plenty of Pennsylvania</u>. New York: H. C. Kinsey and Company, Inc., 1942.

Zielinski, John M. "The Amish in Illinois." <u>Adventure Road</u> 14 (September 1978): 15–17.